Advance Praise for *Anaton*

"*Anatomy of a Survivor* will immediately inform my work with military veterans. Joyce and I met (by chance or fate) in 2015 and have become both friends and colleagues. I have leaned on her many times since, incorporating her insights on recovery and posttraumatic growth in my work with military veterans at the Sierra Club and elsewhere. This book clearly articulates that when faced with trauma, the scariest and biggest challenges in life are the unknowns but we can take control and use this as an opportunity to grow from the experience and return to a life with a greater sense of purpose and belonging. Expertly supported using peer-reviewed research, decades of client observations, and stories of trauma survivors, her descriptive writing style allows the reader to experience a survival journey that culminates in a deeper and more meaningful understanding of the metahabilitated survivor and posttraumatic growth. *Anatomy of a Survivor* should be a primary source for anyone working with trauma survivors and their families."

—**Lt. Col. Aaron M. Leonard,** USA (Ret),
Sierra Club Military Outdoors

"My working relationship with Dr. Mikal-Flynn began over five years ago, through a collaboration with University of California, Davis Comprehensive Cancer Center. Her MetaHab course for clinicians was an eye opener and proved to be the catalyst for me personally as a former cancer researcher, cancer caregiver, cancer survivor and in my work in cancer support with the American Cancer Society. Joyce is able to articulate the deep emotions and effects that trauma drags along with it. She understands through her own story, but better yet, she understands the ways in which the person feeling damaged can look at the scars in a different way, find meaning and gratitude, and access the illusive resilience that often feels just out of reach. While each of us feel our personal trauma solely; there are common tools that, when consistently used, can break us free to find our strength and grow healthier, steadier. It is my absolute pleasure to recommend *Anatomy of a Survivor* to everyone who continues to find meaning and perseverance through trauma."

—**Treasa McPherson**, Cancer Control Strategic
Partnerships Manager, American Cancer Society

"This book is essential for anyone working in trauma recovery. In partnership with other noted experts in the field, Dr. Joyce Mikal-Flynn weaves her own personal story of survival, and the inspiring stories of many others, with the latest neuroscience on post-traumatic growth. She explores the process of healing from trauma in a way that is non-prescriptive, yet still provides a meaningful, evidence-based roadmap to recovery. As a Certified Clinical Trauma Professional, I will definitely be adding this to my resource list for both clients and professionals in order to help create a context of hope on their journey towards resilience and growth."

—**Dr. Christine Lynn Norton**, LCSW, CCTP, CCAT, CET,
Professor, Texas State University, Founder of
Foster Care Adventure Therapy Network

"Since Dr. Mikal-Flynn's first book in 2012, *Turning Tragedy Into Triumph*, I've experienced two traumatic events: the sudden brain surgery for my wife and the cardiac arrest of my father as we sat across from each other eating lunch. My wife and father survived their life-altering events and were greatly aided by her book. With these experiences, I also felt like a survivor. In her latest book, *Anatomy of a Survivor*, Dr. Mikal-Flynn refers to people like me as vicarious and secondary trauma survivors. In simple terms and with the latest research, she explains not just how victims of trauma can survive and thrive from their experience but how family members and friends can too."

—**Rich Hanna**, Owner, Capital Road Race Management,
Sacramento Running Association Hall of Fame Member,
Race Director, Run to Feed the Hungry

"A leading expert on surviving adversity, challenges and troubling experiences Dr. Joyce Mikal-Flynn shows you how to use major traumatic events to survive, but more importantly, to thrive—changing your life and choosing the way you want it to be shaped through the experience. Her words aren't just to 'tell you' but rather to show you how to effectively take on hardships and employ them as powerful growth experiences. This is the book for you to regain the inner belief and self-confidence needed to survive, adapt, and grow from adversity, challenges, and trauma. She explains, in understandable terms, the natural abilities that support your capacity for resilience and growth after survival. Here's your guidebook. After reading *Anatomy of a Survivor*, share the stories, what you learned, applying her ideas first to yourself and then to your loved ones."

—**Sally Edwards**, Author of *Elite Athlete*, Founder, FLEET FEET Sports, CEO and Owner, Heart Zones USA, Triathlon Hall of Fame

"Dr. Joyce Mikal-Flynn has turned a life experience into her passion and has changed how we as recreational therapists now approach tragic life experiences with our clients. She has captured the human experience and translated it to science so that we as health care professionals can improve the overall quality of life for individuals living with disabling conditions. As her former running partner and colleague at Sacramento State I am in constant awe of the impact Dr. Mikal-Flynn has had on students, faculty, and the health care profession. I am excited to include this as a required textbook for my graduate students."

—**Jennifer Piatt,** PhD, CTRS, FDRT, Associate Professor, Indiana University Bloomington School of Public Health

"When thinking about my own challenges and reading *Anatomy of a Survivor*, I was so impressed with how Dr. Joyce skillfully covered all the issues survivors and their families go through with tough, traumatic life events. She addressed the problems clearly and honestly, offering encouragement and great solutions regarding what brings people forward. The stories she provides are awesome, the advice, from my perspective, is perfect and she does it in such an easy to read manner. Thanks, Dr. Joyce, for giving us such an important book—so necessary at this time!"

—**Damon West**, Keynote Speaker, Professor of Criminal Justice, and Bestselling Coauthor of *The Coffee Bean* and *The Change Agent*

"With great courage and resilience, Dr. Joyce Mikal-Flynn triumphantly forged a path out of darkness and explains in compelling detail how she found opportunity in adversity. She shares her hard-earned lessons with grace and offers data and guidance to help others navigate their own path forward. Wherever you are on your personal journey and whatever challenges you may be facing, Dr. Mikal-Flynn offers insightful ideas and practical tools to progress mentally, emotionally, and physically to achieve a life rich in purpose and meaning."

—**Kitty O'Neal**, News Anchor, Newsradio KFBK, Sacramento, Northern California, iHeartMedia Markets Group

"Understandably, you probably spend a great deal of effort trying to avoid pain, struggle and trauma. It makes sense. Unfortunately, no matter your best efforts, you won't be successful. Trauma and tragedy will strike. But it doesn't have to define you. In fact, in her wonderfully readable and well-researched book, Dr. Joyce Mikal-Flynn explains how trauma can be your greatest teacher, leading you toward a life of purpose and meaning. Let this book be your companion as you discover how to turn your trauma into triumph."

—**Joe Sikorra**, Marriage and Family Therapist and Author of *Defying Gravity*

"Dr. Joyce Mikal-Flynn's story of overcoming personal tragedy is riveting. But what makes her book, *Anatomy of a Survivor*, a must-read is how she takes the lessons she learned and turns them into deep and meaningful help for others who have faced similar trauma. 'First and foremost,' she writes, 'this book emphasizes our strengths and capabilities for surviving trauma and mounting a positive productive response in the aftermath. You will learn and fully understand how to use your challenges and trauma to build resilience, grit and growth.' On that simple, yet profound promise, Dr. Mikal-Flynn fully delivers. I highly recommend this book."

—**Bob Dunning**, Daily Columnist, The Davis Enterprise, Host, The Bishop's Radio Hour

ANATOMY OF A SURVIVOR

BUILDING RESILIENCE, GRIT, AND GROWTH AFTER TRAUMA

DR. JOYCE MIKAL-FLYNN

FOREWORD BY: **DAVE MCGILLIVRAY**

Director of the Boston Marathon

Post Hill
PRESS

A POST HILL PRESS BOOK

ISBN: 978-1-64293-727-5
ISBN (eBook): 978-1-64293-728-2

Anatomy of a Survivor:
Building Resilience, Grit, and Growth After Trauma
© 2021 by Dr. Joyce Mikal-Flynn
All Rights Reserved

Cover Design by Marc Cruz

Post Hill Press, LLC
New York • Nashville
posthillpress.com

Published in the United States of America
1 2 3 4 5 6 7 8 9 10

To my grandparents, Keenan and Mary Joyce Burns, and my parents, Jude and Mary Joyce Mikal, for instilling in me an amazing strength of spirit, resilience, and grit, and for providing a model of how to take life on and become stronger after challenges and trauma.

To my husband Terry and my children Elizabeth, Catherine, and Keenan, on that pool deck that day, you were there supporting me and have done so for all these years. You have all saved me, held me up, and helped me in so many ways. Inspired by how you took on your own challenges and struggles, I learned resilience, grit, and how to become better and stronger. Also, I did not survive, recover, or write this book on my own. It was and is a family endeavor, with each of you helping, supporting, and motivating me along the way. Thank you.

To Jennifer K. Gonzales Shushereba, and her and T.J.'s daughter Cecilia Rose. So much was taken; so much was lost. I am committed to keep your work, service, and spirits alive. Thank you for all you have given me and those we served together.

There are only two ways to live your life.
One is as though nothing is a miracle.
The other is as though everything is a miracle.
—Albert Einstein

CONTENTS

I saw the angel in the marble and carved until I set him free.
—Michelangelo

PART ONE

PART TWO

PART THREE

PART FOUR

APPENDICES

Content Contributors: Drs. Sharon Furtak, John D. McPherson, Richard Tedeschi, Serge Campeau, and Erin Skiffer. Catherine W. Schweikert, MPH, PA-C; doctoral candidate. Sally Phelps, LMFT; and Captain Ryan Tweltridge; Sacramento City Fire Department
Writing Contributors: Erin Ryan and Tupper Hull
With deep appreciation for the gift of your time, insight, and ongoing support of my work and this book: Drs. Bridget Parsh, Dean Elias, Louise Timmer, and Robyn Nelson.

FOREWORD

In 2013, two homemade bombs detonated near the finish line of the 117th Boston Marathon, an event I have been the race director for twenty years. Three people died and hundreds were injured, including seventeen who lost limbs.

In the days and months that followed that horrific act of terror, I struggled with exactly how to respond—both personally and professionally. My family was in the crowd near the finish line when the bombs exploded but fortunately all were unhurt. As Race Director for the Boston Marathon—an event at the pinnacle of world-class running since 1897—I was uncertain if we would be able to survive and recover. It was a challenging time. A time of doubt, anxiety, depression.

A year later, on Patriots Day 2014, the 118th running of the Boston Marathon became a historic event. More than 36,000 runners competed officially—9,000 more than the previous year. An estimated one million spectators lined the 26.2-mile route—twice the normal number—in an epic celebration of support, pride, courage, and resilience.

Today, the Boston Marathon is much more than a running event. It has become a symbol of community, recovery, strength, and pride.

I first met Dr. Joyce Mikal-Flynn in the summer of 2013 and have come to admire and respect the work she has done on recovery and resilience. More than that, she has become a friend who has her own remarkable story of personal trauma, recovery, and growth.

Dr. Mikal-Flynn helped me process the tragedy and pain of the 2013 bombings as I navigated the three phases of recovery she identified—survive, adapt, amaze.

We survived. We didn't just recover. We became stronger.

We adapted and became safer.

We amazed by coming back in 2014 and pulling off one of the most epic marathons of all time.

Dr. Mikal-Flynn's guidance and wisdom personally helped me through this process. I owe her a debt of gratitude for her kindness and friendship. Her book will help you in building your personal strength and resilience as well as finding how to grow in the aftermath of trauma. Stay strong and continue to lead the way.

—Dave McGillivray, director of the Boston Marathon

INTRODUCTION

Our world—our globe, communities, friends, families, and ourselves as individuals—are under enormous stress and trauma these days. A global pandemic, economic dislocation and despair, climate change, and fractured communities—how we address these pressures and hardships may well be the greatest challenges of our time. With the right tools and firm determination, you will not only survive these difficult times, you can and will come through them and thrive, becoming stronger, smarter, and more resilient to face tomorrow's challenges.

This is a book about how to effectively deal with and *use* hardships, adversities, and even major traumatic events in a productive, positive manner and over time, bring about resilience, grit, and growth. Little time is spent on reviewing the science regarding *if* people can experience something positive after bad situations. The evidence shows they do. This phenomenon has been identified, researched, and accepted in spiritual practices, philosophies, historical and current events, books, films, and documentaries.

Stop for a moment. Think about it. You most likely have already faced adversity, either minor or significant, and after a time, used it as motivation to improve, learning a valuable lesson that helped you become stronger and more resilient. This response didn't occur in spite of the challenge but as a direct result of it. You experienced what is called *adaptive resilience, metahabilitation*, and *posttraumatic growth* (*PTG*). These terms have been coined and studied for years by myself and Drs. Lawrence Calhoun, Richard Tedeschi, and Serge Campeau. PTG has been recognized and described by Calhoun and Tedeschi as the potential for positive psychological, cognitive, and behavioral changes experienced in the aftermath of a traumatic event or a struggle with a major life crisis. Dr. Campeau's work shows how habituation and learned stress responses brought about by lesser or minor hardships can engage your brain and emotional systems to support and foster resilience and adaptability—a mainstay of PTG.

My work dovetails on both of these ideas. I describe the makeup of a survivor and detail a strengths-based rehabilitation model called metahabilitation, which guides and shows you how to move through troubling and traumatic events to build resilience and grit and move forward, surviving, adapting, and eventually growing in the aftermath of challenges and traumas.

First and foremost, this book emphasizes your strengths and capabilities for surviving trauma and mounting a positive productive response in the aftermath. Next, it will help you recognize how you use challenges, as well as significant hardships, to become resilient and stronger, even if you were unaware of doing so. Finally, it will detail *how* survivors of significant traumatic events can and do move forward and, over time, experience PTG. Using stories and insights, up-to-date research, and behavioral science, this book reveals what motivated and supported people in their choice and mindset to move forward—the *why*. More importantly, neuroscience, neurobiology, genetics, and psychology will show you the *how*. Guidance and a specific strengths-based recovery system and model—metahabilitation—will reveal exactly how individuals who face such situations not only survive, but—with a sliver of hope, time, and great effort—thrive as a direct result of the event. Using those experiences, supported by science and research, you will learn and fully understand how to use your challenges and traumas to build resilience, grit, and growth.

I'm writing as a researcher who studies trauma and what builds resilience and growth afterward, but I also have a deep personal connection to the subject matter. In 1990, after a sudden and unforeseen cardiac event, I died, and for over twenty minutes, doctors provided

CPR, eventually returning me to life. I came back. I was alive, but I would come to find that this new life wasn't my life at all. As with other survivors, I faced depression, grief, fear, numerous unanswered questions, overwhelming personal and professional setbacks, and what seemed like insurmountable obstacles. It took time, stamina, and humility before I ultimately came to realize that this event was not an end point but a beginning. It wasn't overnight, but over time I recognized that taking control of my life started with making the critical choice to move forward. Once that choice was made, there was no turning back. My struggle wasn't something to get over, but something that fueled me. At every obstacle, failure, setback, and misstep, I constantly reminded myself, *you got this*. I eventually accepted that this new life wasn't my old life, and if I pushed myself, I could make something even better. It was really up to me.

I remembered making similar decisions in the past and how I was able to effectively deal with and overcome minor troubling life challenges. But this situation was overwhelming—almost impossible. I suffered major assaults and disruptions to my physical, intellectual, emotional, and spiritual systems. Initially, I couldn't remember my husband and children, and I got confused in my own home and lost in my neighborhood. I was—using an unsophisticated medical term—a mess. Mixed up, angry, and scared, I had no idea what life was left for me. Frightened and unsure of my future, I was in a deep, dark void with little idea of how to crawl out; however, I was determined to do so. With time and great effort and support from family, friends, and clinicians, I recognized very specific behaviors and mindsets that were needed to work through this situation.

I surrendered. I asked for and accepted help. I continually focused on what I could do, taking as much control over my life as possible, adapting when I needed to, but also setting goals for my future. I eventually got some traction in my life and started moving forward. Later, with more time and effort, I found meaning in my pain, rebuilt a life, and found my purpose helping others find their courage, strength, and wisdom in the aftermath of crises. I created both a word and rehabilitation system, metahabilitation, to describe and guide others in their journey through the tough, frightening, and unsure times after trauma.

The Setup

This book is arranged using a foreword and an introduction, followed by four parts. The foreword by Dave McGillivray, director of the Boston Marathon, gives you an idea of how my work helped him during the traumatic and trying times involving the bombings at the 2013 marathon. The introduction provides an overview of concepts and goals and explains the four parts of this book.

Part One begins with the necessity, the importance of this book, my unique capabilities and background to author this book, followed by "My Story," which explains how it all began with my story, my brush with death.

Part Two covers the supportive evidence, the foundational science and research; how and what goes into the makeup of a survivor, including psychology, genetics, epigenetics, posttraumatic growth, and the neuroscience of stress, resilience, happiness, and gratitude.

Part Three details the anatomy of a survivor along with a virtual "how to". These chapters reveal how to use the strengths-based system, metahabilitation, to survive, adapt, and grow after trauma.

Finally, Part Four provides content on wellness and mindfulness strategies and a conclusion. It is good practice to be fully aware of what you are already doing to take care of yourself while understanding *why* these activities and mindsets are important, and *how* they work. Also, I suggest a few new ones you might want to try.

Through endurance we conquer.
—Ernest H. Shackleton

From reading this book, I want you to:

- Recognize your resilience and strength. You are here, you are a survivor, and you are tough. *You got this!*
- Recognize your internal and external mechanisms and systems that respond and successfully deal with adversities, challenges, and traumas.
- Understand how life's challenges, struggles, and disappointments build resilience and support positive behaviors that encourage posttraumatic growth (PTG).
- Appreciate and use metahabilitation, a strengths-based recovery system to guide you and your family in managing and moving forward during and after both minor and major challenges and traumatic events.
- Understand the use of the Metahab system in a clinical and therapeutic setting.

After reading this book, I hope you recognize, first in yourself then in others, how tough and resilient you are. Know that your troubling, traumatic experiences have, over time, helped you become stronger and more resilient. *You choose.* You ultimately can and do make the choice regarding the direction you want to go, the path to take. Sometimes you can make it on your own, and sometimes you need extra help to move forward. I needed help and extra support. That assistance, guidance, and support reveals your thoughtful and pragmatic insight and strength. *You got this!*

A Reminder...

I understand that readers of this book are in unique and personal places as they read about the challenges of traumatic experiences and what is involved in the healing journey. You may passionately agree with everything, question some of it, or disagree with parts. I suggest that it is useful and helpful to read it more than once, and at different times and transitions in your healing process. My purpose is to provide specific ideas and valuable information that resonates and supports your recovery and growth over time.

Let me give you an example. Cassidy is a person I came to know after she read my first book and through our work together. In her early thirties she suffered a stroke, causing her to lose movement on the left side of her body. She lives in Italy, but a friend of hers in the U.S. heard me speak, told Cassidy about my research, and sent her my first book *Turning Tragedy Into Triumph*. Cassidy later reached out to me and thanked me for the book and my research. We were able to meet in person a few years later and she laughed as she shared with me that after initially reading that book, she became angry and "threw it across the room," frustrated with what she read. However, several months later she picked it up again, and at this time in her healing process, she was ready. She could not put it down; now it made complete sense to her. She understood the process and recognized that my work, research, and the metahabilitation recovery system helped unearth and supported her resilience, grit, and ultimate growth. Cassidy and I became friends. She invited me to Italy, and I stayed with her and her family when I presented my work and research at the very rehabilitation center she attended in the aftermath of her trauma.

Take your time reading this work. You will readily agree with some of it, and some of it may initially make you frustrated like Cassidy. But stay with it. The goal is to provide support and get you to think about and recognize how strong you are. Use insights from prior adversities and challenges and identify how they helped make you better. You have amazing systems that protect and allow you to effectively deal with future troubling and traumatic situations. I want this book to guide and inspire you. Trust yourself. Believe in yourself. *You got this!*

"See you on the other side."

A few days before submitting this manuscript, my son Keenan called.

"I don't want to bother you. Just checking in. How are you doing with the book?"

"Great," I answered, "basically done. In the next seventy-two hours, I am going to review it one more time, add the finishing touches, and get ready to send it in." We talked a little more about the content of the book, what I learned during this process, and how kind and helpful people were in providing guidance and support.

"Sounds good. I am proud of you. Keep it up and see you on the other side," he said.

The next day when I was on my run—something I do before I write—I smiled and thought about that line, "see you on the other side." I like it. That simple phrase actually says and means a lot to me; it references a journey. Planned and sometimes unplanned, this saying indicates a before and after, the completion of a project, mission, or journey and all the meaning, knowledge, wisdom, trials, and tribulations that are a part of that accomplishment—*making it to the other side* of a test or challenge.

I feel like I have made it to a lot of "other sides" in my life. This book is definitely one of them. It may have taken a few months to write, but it is the culmination of a significant life event, over two decades of rigorous, intense reflection, thought, and research, years of experiences, insights, investigation, collaboration, learning new things, and hours of contemplation. An incredible amount of time and effort has gone into this work. Feeling a duty to learn, study, and bring forth significant information to help those who have suffered has been worth it. This book is the peak of a very important journey to get it right and get this information to you. You have systems in place that respond and support your survival, adaptation, and growth, allowing you to become better and stronger. The paradox is that much of the time, you don't actually recognize these abilities until you are tested and get to the "other side."

Enjoy the book. Read the stories. Review the research. Pay attention to the observations, ideas, and suggestions regarding productive recovery and rehabilitation. Recognize what goes into the makeup of a survivor and what builds resilience and grit. Find out how to take your adversity and grow to become the master of your fate. *You got this.* See you on the other side of your journey!

PART ONE

CHAPTER 1

WHY THIS BOOK, WHY ME?

Tough, traumatic times are part of reality, but recently our country and our world has been significantly affected by incredibly challenging times. We need this book. I can help; this book can help. I have dedicated over two decades of my life to the study of trauma, focusing on what brings forth a productive recovery. It is personal. I understand it, seeing firsthand how my trauma affected me and my family physically, socially, cognitively, and spiritually. I know the despair and depression that comes with life-altering events. I lived it. I get it. I appreciate the fear of having little to no control of one's life and feeling completely frustrated by a lack of awareness and guidance toward a potentially positive outcome.

Everything I experienced—the good and the bad—every mountain I climbed informed me, shaped me, revealed to me, and taught me about myself and what could be accomplished after trauma. My personal frustration fueled my clinical work and research, becoming my obsession. I needed to get answers and more clearly understand my situation to move forward and help others. As a healthcare professional—and in an effort to gain insight, understanding, and answers—I even returned to school and earned a master's and a doctorate degree, specifically studying challenges and traumatic events and, more importantly, what survivors *can* do and what supports their ability to become more resilient and grow after trauma.

For years I have been absorbed in this topic, this aspect of the human experience, earning advanced degrees studying, researching, and writing books, articles, book chapters, and workbooks addressing issues and aspects of trauma that influence and guide survivors toward posttraumatic growth. Endless hours were spent in contemplation and observation of survivors who had achieved growth after trauma. I created the term to describe the philosophy and developed a unique and specific system guiding one toward resilience and posttraumatic growth: metahabilitation. Doctoral research helped clarify it as a strengths-based system of recovery with stages that direct survivors toward adaptation, resilience, and posttraumatic growth. I received funding supporting my work and research from the National Institute of Health (NIH); California State University, Sacramento; and the National Collegiate Athletic Association (NCAA) and presented my research findings and this system of recovery in several countries and throughout the U.S. I have addressed schools and educational administrators, healthcare professionals, clinicians and therapists, social workers, veterans, first responders, athletes, coaches, athletic directors, business executives, and multiple recovery and rehabilitation programs. I started a business, Metahab (drjmf.com), and produce a podcast called *Sliver of Hope: Stories of Survival and Growth*, which specifically addresses the gap in recovery, provides a more optimistic viewpoint, and promotes the capacity of survivors to heal and grow after trauma. I have lectured at numerous universities, businesses and conferences and developed a college course called "Traumatology: An Introduction to Posttraumatic Growth," which profiles this philosophy and intervention.

Over the years, through my work and ongoing research, I continually addressed all aspects of trauma, leaving no stone unturned, no aspect of recovery unaddressed. I have personally experienced all the ups and downs of trauma and its aftermath. This book provides that content and is designed to help you, the survivor, find out how to move forward past all the darkness and despair into hope, resilience, and personal strength.

Nobody explained any of this to me. I had to first discover it in myself, and that awareness and knowledge energized me. I couldn't stop. It has been a deep desire and duty to share all I experienced, researched, and learned. My colleague, Dr. Bridget Parsh, continually and supportively reminds me, "This isn't about you. You found out very important information regarding how to deal with trauma. You have to share it!" She is right. My mission is clear: help survivors by sharing my research and that of others, showing mechanisms and specific guidance on how to use hardships and challenges to build resilience, grit, and growth after trauma, and to instill hope in those who encounter and have suffered from life-altering events. I have done the work. Let me save you time, energy, and unnecessary anxiety by providing this research, giving specific directions, and letting you know that there is a *way up* and a *way out* and that the capacity and power to achieve this is already in you. *You got this!*

CHAPTER 2

MY STORY

On July 22, 1990, my heart stopped beating and for more than twenty minutes, I was dead. My life didn't flash before my eyes until much later, when I was facing the loss of myself, even in survival. The more I struggled to recover from the trauma in every layer of my being, the more humble and open I became, and one ordinary memory pushed its way to the front. I was back in my eighth-grade classroom, absorbing the challenge laid down by Sister Grace Marie.

"Students, it is better to aim for the sky and hit the fence than it is to aim for the fence and hit the ground."

Wise as it is obvious. It needs saying because sometimes, we can't see the sky.

Seeds of Survival

My father wasn't there to see my body shudder and sink to the bottom of a pool. A bit of mercy, considering he watched his brother drown. They were just boys, playing in the shallows of Lake Michigan. As his younger sibling paddled farther and farther out, Dad begged him to come back. He was already swimming toward him when he saw the current pull his brother down. Right there and still too late. He suffered silently with this memory throughout his life, but most acutely as he grew up feeling his parents' blame. They weren't particularly loving or kind, and I think it sowed the opposite emotions in my father.

His name was Jude. He was manifestly tough, a Navy man who served in the Korean War and dug deep to give his wife and six children a good life. He didn't lie or suffer fools; he was absolutely authentic in a way that could be withering. But he was just as fierce in showing his love for us and his constant support and pride in our efforts. We could see his devotion to my mother, Mary Joyce, the backbone of the family. She never complained about how tough we had it financially; she just got to work doing what was needed with a grace about her and an intensely determined inner strength. She was unfailingly positive, pleasant, and funny.

As children we joked about Mom making powdered milk and slicing the cheese and turkey so thin for our sandwiches that all we tasted was bread. She knew how to stretch what we had, and she did it with contagious good humor. Every week we loaded into our Volkswagen bus with a bag of those sandwiches, homemade cookies, a jug of lemonade, and just enough money for all six of us to get an ice cream.

Fun was part of our family's foundation, along with education and a commitment to each other and our Catholic faith. No family is perfect, but we had more good times than bad and knew we were loved and safe. My parents worked hard for each of us, clearly making sacrifices to give their children all they could. The second born and the oldest girl, I stepped in a lot to help my mother. I knew how hard it was for her, so I never felt put upon; however, a great deal was expected of me by my parents and myself. Very early on, it was clear that if I wanted something, I always had their amazing support and guidance; I just wouldn't have their financial backing. They would do what they could. I got it. My dreams were in my hands. Plenty slipped through my fingers. I wasn't always successful and had many disappointments, but each accomplishment was a brick in an ever more solid sense of what I could do with my abilities and my parents' absolute faith in me.

After high school, I was admitted to the only college I really wanted to attend, the University of San Francisco. With student loans, scholarship money, and part-time jobs, I worked my way through the school of nursing. My parents set such an example and taught us so much about being of service that I went from graduation straight into a position with Volunteers in Service to America (VISTA). Assigned to a migrant/seasonal healthcare clinic in the Northwest, I thought I was joining a team of public health nurses. When I arrived, I found out that I was *the* public health nurse. Although I had training, I was not prepared to be the only one.

I quickly referred to textbooks, physicians, and other colleagues at the clinic regarding my duties and expectations. It was a steep learning curve, but I was proud of my service to the community of seasonal workers. Their tenacity and adaptability were humbling. I visited camps when parents were working out in the field and saw very young children dutifully caring for each other. That experience has stayed with me throughout my professional life, revealing the personal grit brought forth as they dealt effectively and courageously with adversity.

While working at the clinic, I encountered my first nurse practitioner (NP). The role was relatively new, and I was intrigued at the level of independent decision-making and care she provided. So after my obligation with VISTA was fulfilled, it took two attempts to get into the NP program at the University of California, Davis. I did well in all my studies and clinical practice, and during this time I was fortunate to meet my husband Terry. My eventual career and family kept me challenged and fulfilled. Life came to a place that felt wonderfully packed and right.

It feels that way now. My husband and I have three accomplished, grown children and six beautiful grandchildren. We have weathered many storms over forty years together, but the one that almost took my life was a lightning strike that ignited my whole world.

Prayer on Pavement

In the years leading up to my accident, running was my passion and daily meditation. It helped me stop smoking and reach and maintain a healthy weight. From my physical and mental well-being to my sense of pride, it fed me in so many ways. Knowing how much this activity meant to me—how core it was to my identity—is vital to understanding what I lost. There were times when I fixated on running a little too much and focused on performance rather than the joy of just getting out there with friends. Competing in my first marathon is a good example.

Family Ties to Survival Tools

I encourage people to learn and document their family history. On those weekly trips in the VW bus, as well as spending time with my grandparents, I got to know my family's strength and resilience through stories. I learned about my grandfather, who lost his mother at age six or seven, and was placed in an orphanage. He escaped in his early teens and grew up on the streets of Chicago, surviving by working as a water boy for a company he eventually retired from as vice president. He was one of the most loving, caring people I ever met, and he never talked about himself or his lot in life. My grandmother told his story, along with her own. Born in 1900, she experienced WWI and the Great Depression and raised two successful children. These few pieces of my grandparents' story made me realize we don't need celebrities to be our role models. Amazing examples are closer than you think. Take some time and ask family members to talk about themselves and other relatives; it may lend a colorful perspective to your own strength and resilience.

In the early 1980s, few people were running marathons—certainly not a lot of mothers with young children. While I had been very athletic in my youth and even did some casual running in college, the demands of school, work, and motherhood led me to a normal life without much physical activity. Having two children in fifteen months, working part time, and trying to lose weight and find time to myself, I realized I needed to do something. So I began taking walks. As my pace quickened, I thought, *maybe I could run again....* Not only could I run, I enjoyed it more than walking. It gave me an overall feeling of wellness, improving my weight and providing significant help in managing my anxiety. That is how running became a ritual. As soon as my husband came home from work, out the door I went for a thirty to forty-five-minute run before dinner. I came back a calmer, more cheerful person. The tensions of the day simply melted away, and I felt better equipped to handle all of my responsibilities. Running became central to my social life as well. I joined a club and got my husband into it, and we spent much of our time together and with friends doing this activity I grew to need.

I first contemplated running a marathon while in Fleet Feet, the shop where I bought all my gear. A t-shirt from a past marathon was on display, and I began to think of 26.2 miles as a personal challenge. A week later, I bumped into my friend Kurt. I knew he had run a few marathons, and I asked if he thought I was capable, given that I was a busy wife and mother.

"Of course, you can. And if you want, I can teach you how to run a marathon," he said.

That was it. Someone opened a door. I listened intently, got the books he suggested, and spent time consulting with others who'd completed marathons. Kurt was planning to run one in a few months and suggested I join. I had time to train, and I made the commitment. I didn't plan on a specific time; I just wanted to finish. In 1986, I completed the San Francisco Marathon in a little over four hours. I was hooked on running and the drive to improve. Just a few hours after finishing that first race, I was dissecting and diagnosing my performance. *I really could have done it better and gone faster if I improved my training, nutrition, hydration, and course preparation,* I thought. That aspect of my personality came barreling out: almost an obsession to excel. I wasn't satisfied with my result because I knew I could do better.

I had promised my husband I would only do one marathon just to see if I could finish. But then I had to do one more, just to see if I could finish faster. That was it. He knew it. I set my sights on running longer and stronger. There was something inside me—perhaps beginning in my youth—that whipped me toward the next level to get better, get it right, and be satisfied. Obsessions can improve you, but unbalanced, they can blur or totally obscure your perspective. I didn't know it then, but I lived for a long time without balance, and it took a crisis to open my eyes.

The best times I had running were with my husband and friends, connecting on beautiful trails and sharing the rush of great races. Not satisfied with marathon distance, I got into ultras to push myself. My group began running 50K trail runs to extend our fun. Our children joined in on some of the shorter runs—sometimes running, sometimes riding their bikes alongside. As they got older, going for a run became an amazing time for us to talk. It was all a lifestyle for me. Socialization and fitness were significant aspects, but much deeper than that, running gave me an identity and some of the most spiritual times I have ever experienced.

Pregnant with our third child, I jogged up until the day before his birth and began running again as soon as I could, noting that I was faster after his delivery. That was me, the mother of three who ran marathons. Some people thought what I did was cool, even admirable, while others thought I was crazy. I loved that part of myself. This was my passion, and I worked diligently to become better. Looking for new challenges, I transitioned to short-course and Olympic-distance triathlons. About a month prior to my cardiac event, I participated in a triathlon called the Vineman. The swim was in a lake so murky, I couldn't see my hand stroking through the water. If my heart had stopped while I was swimming there, it would have taken some time to find me, and I would never have written this book.

Life after Death

It was a warm, blue day in July. We were at a championship swim meet—my husband Terry and I with two-year-old Keenan, cheering on his big sisters Elizabeth, eight, and Catherine, seven. It was a two-day event, and the second day involved a fun relay for parents. I gathered a team and insisted on swimming the last leg, as I was the fastest. There was a burst of applause as I touched the wall, then something happened. Terry saw me sink thirteen feet down to the bottom of the pool. He realized I wasn't coming up and was in the water fast, locking his arms around me and swimming me to the surface where, just moments before, my own team had won the race.

A physician named Stuart Gherini had been racing in the lane next to mine, and he helped pull my body onto the pool deck. He noted that I wasn't breathing and didn't have a pulse. He called for help as he began CPR, forcing blood through my vessels to keep my brain alive. Fortunately, a few other parents in the crowd were physicians—Garrett Ryle and an emergency room doctor named Bruce Gordon. Taking turns, they regained a very weak pulse after twenty-two minutes. A rescue helicopter landed in the football field next to the pool and sped me toward the nearest trauma center.

I was thirty-five and an avid marathon runner and triathlete with no personal history of cardiac or respiratory issues. Yet here I was in the ICU on a respirator, having suffered something I shouldn't have suffered. That I survived was just as mystifying. When I woke up, I'm sure it was a dramatic moment for my loved ones, as no one knew how well my brain had come through the trauma. For me, though, those initial moments were too immediate to be scary. I sat up in my hospital bed and saw my brother-in-law and his wife at the end of my bed. I asked where I was, and they explained that I had some sort of cardiac event and was resuscitated. My eyes flicked to my chest then my arms. I had worked as an ICU nurse and was looking for burn marks left by the defibrillator and the telltale bandages from IVs. There were no signs of such an assault on my body.

"That couldn't have happened," I said.

Without arguing, they asked if I wanted anything. My favorite splurge danced in my head—a cheeseburger, fries, and a vanilla milkshake. Only, I couldn't find those words.

"I would like one of those things that has layers to it, with yellow stuff on it and where you drive through a place to get it. It comes with these long things you put salt on and a cup of white cold stuff."

It was hugely encouraging to my medical team that I could express myself at all, but there was obvious damage. Plucking language out of my brain in this state was like being slightly intoxicated, aware of the right words and phrasing but stumbling through some viscous haze to reach them. Mercifully, I was too dazed to fully grasp what was going on, but the next days and weeks brought profound disorientation and unbearable anxiety. Memory loss kept me in the fog. I asked repeatedly what happened to me, and seconds after an explanation, I asked the same question. Initially, I didn't recognize my husband or my children. I was battling cognitive delays and physical limitations, as well as intense anger, severe depression, spiritual angst, and consuming fear. The tests were numerous and painful, but neither they nor the second, third, or fourth opinions could tell my family why this happened. Not one specialist could determine the exact nature or cause of the cardiac arrest or predict with any certainty what my future would hold. They weren't even sure I had a future.

It could have been a shallow-water drowning from respiratory insufficiency, as I probably swam the entire length of the pool without taking a breath. It could have been an electrical malfunction inside my heart. Nothing was definitive. Always advocating for me, Terry finally asked one physician, "If you don't know what happened to her, can you send us to someone who does?"

The more aware I became of what I was facing, the more I pleaded with doctors.

"Can I run? When will I run again? When can I swim again?"

The electrophysiologist in charge of my case specialized in the mechanics and effects of irregular cardiac rhythms told me, "You will walk, but you won't run or swim anymore."

"You don't know who you are talking to," I said. "I have been through a lot in my life and gotten through it. I will get through this. You should never, never take hope away from a person. Just wait. I will come back." I turned in a huff to go back to my room, but I had no idea which direction to walk.

The doctor muttered to a nurse, "She's yelling at me and can't even find her room."

It was hard to believe my own defiant promise when my brain was busy betraying me.

I know this sounds odd, even crazy, but I was more upset about not running than I was about any other aspects of what I survived. Told these activities were going to be taken away, I fell into a very deep, dark hole of despair. Being alive was fantastic, but I wanted—and begged for—the life I had before. I actually demanded to do the things that kept me sane, gave me joy, and defined my identity. I didn't want to hear the word "no." I wanted doctors to tell me "when." When could I live again?

I finished every race I started, even in intense heat or storms. I never walked or stopped until I came to a finish line. Call it tenacity, fixation, or stubbornness, but some doctors told me later that it was this mindset and my level of fitness that made me able to survive and eventually move past my brush with death.

But on this day, after hearing what I feared most, I sat on my hospital bed and sobbed. Terry, afraid of what might happen if I did run or swim again, said, "You are alive. I can't believe you are crying and worried about running again." He didn't get it. No one did. My life transformed in an eye-blink, and I wanted it back. It's tough to think about even now, but life-changing events take time to process. I was at the beginning. The journey toward recovery would take me from intense emotional and spiritual despair, including suicidal ideation, to making the choice to live life on its terms. I had to completely break down to break open.

With time, I understood Terry's point of view. He was the one who dove to the bottom of the pool and brought my lifeless body up. He was facing life with a wife who once had it all under control—the home, the family, a career as a nurse practitioner—and now couldn't remember names of family and friends, struggled to use a microwave, and cried over not being able to run. It was a hard, frightening time for us all, amplified by the fact that no one really knew what happened to me or how to ensure my safety going forward. I just wanted to go back.

My hospital stay lasted almost a month, and when I got home, I didn't recognize it. I had to ask my young daughters, "What outfits and shoes did I like to wear?" In the kitchen, I would look around and ask, "Where did I keep the dishes and the silverware? What meals did I prepare?" I was agitated and exhausted. Friends came over to help care for my children because I literally couldn't.

I did occupational therapy before returning home from the hospital and got angry when I couldn't perform simple tasks. Even heating water in a microwave was suddenly vexingly impossible. Racked with anxiety over countless new limitations, I spun into a very deep depression. Even though I wanted to, initially I couldn't participate in the athletic events I had enjoyed so much in the past due to very real fatigue, the lack of medical clearance, and fear that what had happened once might happen again. To have one of the greatest points of pleasure and pride in my life taken away from me and to constantly dread that any overexertion could result in another cardiac arrest was overpowering. The life I knew dissolved.

I spent most of my days sleeping, and when I did find the energy to go for a walk, I got lost in my own neighborhood. After a week of this, I decided I was not going to let it get the best of me. I was going to run again, despite what the doctors told me. The first time I went out, I made it two blocks. I had to sit on the curb and recover before I limped back home. I was filled with panic, which turned into fury. In the past, I was in charge, the one keeping things going and always organizing everyone's schedule and activities, and now, I could barely do a fraction of what I had done.

A speech therapist came to help me with my aphasia, a loss of ability to clearly articulate and understand the spoken and written word. Scared and frustrated, I blamed her for my problems and refused to continue. With every attempt to resume normal life, I was made more aware of the limitations preventing it. I made a series of poor choices, something I later learned is common in people who have suffered brain trauma. I was caught speeding with my children in the car, a reckless act that was way out of character. My husband saw the ticket and said, "Something is wrong with you. I'm not sure what it is, but we need some help."

I went to a therapist to deal with my depression and get some answers about my behavior. I shared with him that since my cardiac arrest occurred in a very public place, I would be out and about and people would stop me and ask, "Aren't you the woman who had the accident at the pool?" Or they would point at me, saying, "There is that woman who almost died." It was unnerving and weird, like I was some sort of celebrity.

"You are," he said, "but it came with a huge price tag, didn't it?" How right he was.

I had always been so independent. I had come through other troubles and challenges, but this was different. I couldn't do what I was used to doing. I was physically spent much of the time, pissed off and completely angry with God. I was almost entirely dependent on others to make decisions for me. My children and husband had to guide me through daily routines. But nighttime was the worst.

You died, and no one is sure what happened, replayed over and over in my head. *What if it happens again?* I was constantly afraid of death. This was bigger than anything I had dealt with before. I had met my match. And I realized that whatever energy I had now needed to be focused on building some kind of future. It was time to shake off my ego and resentment and move forward.

A second speech therapist came at my request. I began to work in earnest because now, I understood the impact of the brain damage I suffered when my heart stopped doing what it had always done. It affected every part of my life and the lives of those closest to me. I felt isolated, but I did not have to *be* isolated in working through things. Accepting help can be so hard, especially for people like me who are used to being the helpers, but it is pivotal to overcoming trauma rather than just surviving it.

In speaking with my children years later, it was clear that the time and effort my husband, friends, and relatives took in helping me was very influential. My oldest daughter Elizabeth had her birthday ten days after my accident, just as I was being moved from the ICU to another part of the hospital. I saw pictures of friends and their children bringing a surprise party to our house. My circle filled in the gaps so effectively that my children don't remember those times being particularly frightening or out of control. They remember the fun overnights and outings. It didn't faze them when I had to ask how to do simple tasks or find things in our home. They were young and wonderfully adaptable, though it did weigh on them that no one knew what had taken me away and if it would actually occur again.

One night I stayed late visiting a friend, and when I returned home, Elizabeth was furiously doing the dishes and pleading, almost yelling, that I needed to tell people where I was. Despite being insulated by our network, she felt it and grew up fast. I did too, as I recognized my difficulties. I struggled to remember friends' names or exactly how I knew them and hold conversations that had once been effortless. I got lost on streets I had known for more than twenty years. It was absolutely frightening. Pretending I was fine left me wrung out, so I gave in and started being honest about what I couldn't recall. No one judged me; they knew what happened and were supportive and kind. Still, I felt an enormous sense of loss and loneliness in my own mind. Memories came back eventually, but pushing through the void took humility and great effort.

Much of my recovery was self-taught. I used my own ideas to regain my abilities, such as asking professors within the nurse practitioner program I attended if I could sit in and listen during lectures. This was amazingly helpful. In a relaxed atmosphere, I was able to just absorb content and terminology and regain the strategy of the diagnostic process. Using this tactic as well as intense work with a speech and communications therapist, and the unwavering support of my clinical colleagues, allowed me to return to my work as a nurse practitioner. It took some time, but I recognized the traction and the gains I was making. That doesn't mean my trajectory was linear. Even with a strong support system and despite everything I still had after coming so close to death, the journey of recovery often left me feeling utterly alone. I struggled deeply on a soul level. But my desperation to find pathways back to life would later be powerful motivation to tackle the standard system of recovery offered to survivors of trauma. Those systems failed me in countless ways, and I wasn't going to let that stand.

God had also failed me. Like many survivors, I let anger and despair turn me away from the very beliefs that had always helped me cope. I felt let down by the forces I had always trusted and wanted to scream and scream and scream, *Why?!*

I didn't pray after my accident, at least not sincerely. For six months, a sense of impending doom was smoldering, and finally, it blazed into overwhelming fear, fear that this would happen to me again. I could not take it anymore, so I surrendered. I had to. I had no other choice. One night, I got out of bed and down on my knees and pleaded. *God, take these feelings away from me. I cannot live with this fear anymore.* I got back into bed and slept peacefully through the rest of the night. The fear and dread have never returned to that degree.

I say "to that degree" because I struggle even now. It is human to be hopeless in moments, no matter what signs you might receive or how much you learn and evolve. I know this because nine months after my heart stopped, I thought about throwing away my second chance. I was driving home from work, raw from that day and so many others that underlined my losses. I was better and still making gains, but I knew I was not who I once was. The loss of cognitive and physical ability, the holes in my memory, and the lack of control in my life were immensely disturbing, not only for me but for my family. Not being fully aware or informed and not completely knowing of all the ramifications of such loss was almost worse than the loss itself. Frustration and fear filled me as I stared at the darkness on either side of the road.

I can't go on like this. Trying to come back is just too hard. I don't want to live this way. If I drove my car into this embankment, it would all be over

But then, more overwhelming than despair was the realization that I could not do this to the people who had worked so hard to save me. All the medical professionals and therapists, my family and friends who had sacrificed and given so much just to give me a chance—I couldn't do it to them. At that moment, I made a crucial choice and promised to live and continue working at getting better. I have come to identify that decision as foundational for survivors to move forward—an absolute necessity. Survivors can likely tell you the day, time, and place where they resolved to take control of the unknown, of their destiny. For me, it was on that dark road, and I spent the rest of the drive brainstorming how to get myself on track for a useful and productive future. For myself and my family, I would do whatever it took to claw back my life, even if I didn't recognize myself afterward.

Ongoing speech therapy was key. So was finding a cardiologist who was a runner. Dr. Daniel VanHamersveld listened to me and supported my desire to get back into running. The first step was cardiac rehabilitation, where I could experiment with exercise while being monitored and take medication to slow my heart rate. We were going to find out what I could safely do, or at least what loss I needed to make peace with.

Still not completely sure of what happened, my husband advocated for me to see a cardiologist known for his work with electrical problems of the heart known as dysrhythmias. We traveled over two hours to meet him. We wanted to know the precise cause of my cardiac event. He looked at all my files, tests, and labs, asked many questions, then examined me. After all of that, he sat down quietly, looking at my husband then at me.

"First of all, you are the luckiest person I have ever met. I've never met anyone who had that much CPR and lived, and is also sitting up and speaking with me," he said. "And unless someone was inside your heart at that moment, I don't think we will ever really know what happened. But your life has changed forever. And there are decisions about how to live your life, and you need to make them.

"If you want to run again—and that is how things will end for you—that is your decision to make. But I don't think that is what will happen."

This doctor listened to me; he gave me control. On the ride home, I was almost giddy. I had been fighting for so long to get back into running, and I realized I was really fighting people constantly saying no. When he didn't say that, I rethought all of it. I *could* slow down and follow his advice and continue my work with cardiac rehabilitation. By offering me control without judgment, he calmed and opened me to other possibilities. I didn't need to race, I didn't need to push it. I survived, and now the life I had back was mine. Not the one I had before the accident, but a new one, and I had the freedom to begin to decide what that life was going to be.

In cardiac rehab, I walked, then jogged and finally ran. The physical release was incredible, but so was the social support from the nurses, therapists, and other patients. It is absolutely essential to have someone advocate for your care (my husband and cardiologist were in my corner), take as much control over your recovery as possible, and keep focusing on what you *can* do.

A couple years after he said I wouldn't run again, I bumped into the hospital's cardiac specialist. I asked, "Do you remember me?" "Oh, yes, I remember you—vividly." Pleased to hear how much better I'd gotten since losing my way in the hall outside my room, he then told me I was one of the bravest women he had ever met.

Leaning Way In

Slowly, I found my way back into the world. I got outside with friends who were happy to slow the pace of running for me. And I participated more fully in my children's school events and social activities, gaining a deeper appreciation for everyday pleasures.

As I settled back into my work as a nurse practitioner, I felt I needed to do more. I had questions that wove my own experience together with the larger issue of what rehabilitation models failed to address: Was this what survival looked like? Did others feel depressed, anxious, and angry? What more could and should be done to help people after trauma?

So, two years after my event, I decided to go back to school for a master's degree in nursing and study survivors of death events. My return to school would hopefully accomplish a few things. First, I needed to gain confidence and improve my memory and reading and writing skills. I figured pushing myself in a formal classroom setting, something I always loved, would help me do that. I also wanted to know if others who had faced death and been resuscitated had experienced the same troubling aftermath as I had—depression, anxiety, loss of control, confusion, and fear. It turns out I was not alone. My research and others in the field reported the same or similar outcomes.

Life is so interesting. When looking at schools to apply to, I visited Sacramento State University. The chair of the School of Nursing, Dr. Robyn Nelson, happened to walk by as I was speaking with a receptionist. She heard me share my reservations about completing the curriculum because I had been in an accident that caused brain injury. I had significantly improved, but entering an advanced degree program was not going to be easy. Dr. Nelson stopped and asked my name. As soon as she heard it, she froze.

"Are you the woman who drowned at the swim championships?" she asked.

"Yes."

"I was there," she said.

We talked about that day, my life now, and what I was hoping to do. Eighteen months later I earned a master's degree in nursing, completing my research and a thesis: *A Phenomenological Investigation of Near-Death Event Survivors.* I found that survivors of sudden death had much in common, both in terms of struggle and in successfully coping.

Dr. Nelson was my adviser on the project, and she later hired me as an assistant professor. My event brought us together in many ways. She is a loving friend and trusted mentor, one who helped guide my ideas and work as I pursued a doctorate ten years after earning my master's.

I was driven to apply my research in clinical settings, and I needed more data and proof of concept to show the establishment a program that would simultaneously help patients more and reduce the cost and use of care. It was personal for me because I was still unsettled after my admittedly remarkable recovery. From clinical and personal points of view, I felt that the information and interventions offered to me were insufficient in facilitating a complete physical and cognitive recovery. More importantly, the interventions failed to address the event itself as a unique opportunity for emotional, mental, and spiritual growth. I knew there was more; I experienced this growth and recognized it many times in patients I cared for as I resumed my practice, as well as in books and films. There seemed to be a common insight that such events could give more than they took away. What prompted this unique human behavior? What was involved in the power of the human spirit, and how could it be intentionally tapped?

Answering these questions became my obsession. I absolutely needed to know more about this situation, not only for me but to ultimately help others. I believed that understanding our power might open the door to a new way of thinking about and using catastrophic experiences by revealing how they bring forth a deeper appreciation of oneself and life in general. That entailed further investigation and a formal study of why and how these critical life events can and do prompt significant growth and development.

I entered a doctoral program at St. Mary's College with the unambiguous intent to investigate enhanced survivorship. I was assigned an adviser to help direct my studies, but shifting teaching opportunities landed me with a different one. My research also shifted to post-cardiac events and rehabilitation. It was worthwhile, but it was not what I entered the program to do.

Then I was assigned yet another adviser. I met with Dr. Dean Elias to discuss my project, presenting him with over one hundred pages of work on post-cardiac care. We talked for a long while, going over the specifics of what needed to be done. Just before leaving the meeting, I said, almost as an afterthought, "Here is a paper I wrote for a research class. It's an idea I have about rehabilitation; it's called metahabilitation, a word and concept I've been working on. It has to do with the belief that when a person is faced with a catastrophic or deleterious life event, they have the capacity to actually grow and become stronger as a direct result."

He knew my backstory and took the paper. One week later, we met again to firm up the details of my cardiac research. He looked directly at me and said, "You know, this cardiac work is interesting, but this metahabilitation concept is amazing. This is what you need to do."

I was not happy about the prospect of scrapping my work and starting over. Nonetheless, I took some time and really thought about it. He was right. This was my passion. This was where everything was rooted.

After much exploration, collaboration, consultation, and deliberation, the concept and model of metahabilitation crystallized in my dissertation, *Transforming Life Crisis: Stories of MetaHabilitation After Life Crisis*. It was the foundation for my first book and my ongoing research. My family threw me a lovely party to acknowledge its completion. Many friends were there, including a few of the doctors who brought me back to life on that warm July day. Bruce Gordon was among them. I'd run into him many years earlier, not long after my release from the hospital following my accident. He'd asked me how I was doing. At the time I said, "You know, Bruce, I think I have some brain damage." He smiled and said in his reassuring way, "Joyce, I have never resuscitated anyone for that long who actually walked up to me and said, 'I have brain damage.' Keep going. All those neurons in your brain are still there; they are just not firing fast enough yet. You are an athlete. Just like when you have to rehab a sports injury, you have to rehab your brain." As soon as he said it, I understood, and I worked doggedly to do just that.

At my doctoral celebration, after I publicly thanked people and briefly discussed my dissertation and ongoing research, Bruce walked up behind me and whispered, "You know that brain damage you had? I think it's gone!" He smiled, and I knew the journey had been completely worth it.

Joy Comes

Today, I am happy. Of course, I am still presented with other major challenges, from financial struggles and family illnesses to the deaths of both my parents. But I also watched both my daughters marry wonderful men; and my son, who was a baby when I almost left him forever, is marrying a lovely woman later this year. My husband of over forty years and I have been blessed with many grandchildren.

Before my death and slow rebirth, I judged myself only by what I had accomplished—how fast I could run or how much I could squeeze into a day, spending little or no time enjoying it. I failed to prioritize what was essential for a healthy life. Even with limited time and other responsibilities, I never said no to anyone's demands or requests for help. This way of living left me exhausted and frustrated, and I strongly believe it may have brought about my accident. I tended to focus on what I was missing.

Now I see things in a different light. I consider every day a gift and rarely get through one without stopping to appreciate the fact that I am alive and able to share my life with family and friends. I continue to focus on what I can do, listening to advice from doctors but tempering it with my own desires and an awareness of my abilities. I was given back my life—a very meaningful, purposeful, and fulfilling life—something I had been told not to expect.

I remember when I reached my fiftieth birthday, I initially lamented being that old! But when I went on my run, I began to switch my perspective, and rather than bemoaning my age, I celebrated it. Fifteen years before, I was lucky to return to life. I recognized my good fortune and was elated that I was able to *be* fifty.

I continue to research and teach at Sacramento State University, where I created a course based on my findings: *Traumatology: An Introduction to Posttraumatic Growth*. I have a business, Metahab (drjmf.com), and a podcast (*Sliver of Hope, Stories of Survival and Growth*) that help survivors, their families, clinicians, and therapists. I am still running and have completed several marathons and half-marathons over the years, as well as a handful of triathlons. I couldn't participate at the same level as before, and it didn't matter. I am alive. The joy comes not from how fast I run but from the running, the doing, being with people I love. I think about my life so differently. I am awed by the power of the human spirit and the strength of my own will. These are the gifts I was given and continue to receive.

I think often about a quote from the book *Miracle in the Andes* by Nando Parrado. It documents a young rugby team's plane crash in the mountains on their way to a game in Chile. Only a few survived, and they were stranded on a glacier for months before two survivors braved forty-five miles of frozen wilderness to get help. Nando was one of them. His father, thinking the whole time that his son had been killed, met him at the hospital and said, "The sun will come up tomorrow and the day after that and the day after that. Don't let this be the most important thing that ever happens to you. Look forward. You will have a future. You will have a life."

I do have a life, and with that life I try daily to make a difference for others who have suffered, no matter the scope of their trauma. I believe in you. I believe in the human spirit, the human capacity to take on life. I have been incredibly impressed, amazed, humbled, and emotionally overwhelmed by seeing how individuals have taken some of the toughest life situations, some of the worst challenges and traumas, and overcome them to the point of giving back. My story is presented so you'll understand why I do this work and wrote this book and to help you reflect on the nature, disposition, and components of a survivor.

Tough stuff happens. Inherent in your makeup are systems that allow you to survive, adapt, and amaze—to build resilience and grit and grow, not in spite of trauma but as a direct result of it. If you have identified the anatomy of a survivor through my story, apply it to yourself. Analyze your internal structures, your makeup, how you are built, and recognize where your resilience, grit, and growth are generated.

This insight is fundamental. These events force you to look inside and see what you are made of, your capacity. Where do capacities and characteristics come from? How can you effectively engage and use pre-existing systems to navigate and effectively move through hard times? What will make you stronger?

Look at your heritage, people in your past and present who believe in you, pushed and motivated you to go further than you thought you could. Also—and this is important—look at times you fell short. No doubt disappointment and failure have driven you to learn and boldly act at the next opportunity. Success leads to more success. That is when you come up the best and strongest. *You got this.*

After sharing my story, let me introduce you to Part Two of this book where science is the focus. In the following chapters, supportive research is provided revealing the usefulness of stress, the neurobiology of happiness and gratitude, the role that genetics and epigenetics play in trauma and resilience, and finally, the concept and practice of posttraumatic growth. Enjoy the content. Although some of it is dense, I feel it is essential and foundational to understand why and how specific behaviors allow you to survive, adapt, and amaze—to grow in the aftermath of adversities and trauma.

PART TWO

PART TWO

CHAPTER 3

THE POTENTIAL FOR GROWTH—RETHINKING STRESS: CAN IT BE BENEFICIAL?

Life is not always a matter of holding good cards,
but sometimes, playing a poor hand well.
—Jack London

Stress gets a bad rap. Often, when you're asked, "How are you?" you may quickly respond, "I am so stressed!" We hear those words and immediately think negatively because we are programmed to view stress as harmful; however, it is important to recognize that this is not always the case. There are different types of stressors or pressures, and we have amazing systems to deal with all of them. Dr. János Hugo Bruno "Hans" Selye termed the stimulus, *the stressor,* and the response, *the stress.* We are equipped with automatic and natural responses to handle stressful conditions. These systems permit adaptation and adjustments, encouraging improvements to deal effectively with current stresses, while guarding against future threats—developing stress resilience.

Stressors and Stress

Stressors are situations and conditions that challenge one's physical, spiritual, and psychological well-being. The resulting stress is actually the normal and natural response to the increased demand on a body's systems. It is the reaction to situations and events perceived as challenging that tests the many layers of your well-being, causing increased physical and intellectual demands. Think about stressors in this way: running, working out, cycling, getting sick with a cold, taking on a new job or a new position at work, or starting back to school. The response to these activities is the stress. The good news is you have a variety of systems in place to help handle these situations. Your heart and lungs get better at pumping blood and getting oxygen to where it needs to be, your immune system goes into action producing cells to help you fight off the infection, and your brain amps up and becomes activated to help you learn new things, handle new events, and solve problems.

Brief Overview of the Stress System: Autonomic Nervous System

Think back to your high school science days. You might remember studying the autonomic nervous system (ANS). Supplying all the body's organs with needed elements and energy, including blood vessels, heart, lungs, gut, liver, kidneys, bladder, and skin (sweat glands), this system helps with activities to respond appropriately to the inside and outside environments—automatically. We don't even think about it. The two main divisions of the ANS are called *sympathetic* and *parasympathetic*, and both work in special ways to keep you alive and well.

You may know these as the "fight or flight" (or fight and flee) system (sympathetic) and the "rest and digest" system (parasympathetic).

Generally, the parasympathetic division regulates the body's work under relaxed or normal situations. This rest and digest system helps conserve and restore energy, calms or slows the heart rate, and decreases blood pressure. It stimulates the digestive tract, helping to process and digest food. If you engage in relaxation and mindfulness practices, you are using the parasympathetic branch of the ANS.

The sympathetic division prepares and helps the body deal with stressful or emergency situations: to fight or flee the scene to survive. I remember it by thinking how our body has compassion or "sympathy" for us. It wants to make sure we can deal effectively with real and imagined threats. When you are under significant pressure and get nervous and fearful, this system responds to help you survive that emergency or stressful situation. Heart rates, breathing rates, and muscular strength increases, palms sweat, and pupils dilate—all responses that put you on high alert and prepare you to fight or flee. Activities such as digestion and urination are less important during an emergency or life-threatening event and are decreased. (This makes sense. Sometimes after a sporting event, athletes may vomit. During the "fight," their gut or GI system shuts down, and when it is all over, digestion begins again and they may respond by vomiting what was in their stomach before the event.)

It is important to understand that the brain itself doesn't really know if the stressor or danger is real or part of your imagination. That is how scary movies and books work! We need the rational, intellectual, more advanced part of our brain, the frontal lobe, to help evaluate whether it is an immediate danger or something happening farther away because our bodies will react the same whether it is a thought or a physical reality. This plays a role in individuals suffering from anxiety and stress disorders, including PTSD.

Types of Stress

Now that you understand what stress and anxiety can do to the body, let's review the different types of stress—and they aren't all negative. The American Psychological Association defines three types of stress: acute, episodic acute, and chronic. Each type can cause emotional and physical problems and illnesses, but as you will read further, they can also encourage and be used to build resilience, mental strength, and fitness. Work project deadlines, the near miss of a traffic accident, taking a test, or a goalkeeper stopping a shot are just some examples of acute stress. These events require you to be more focused and attentive, and your system responds and helps by increasing your heart and respiratory rate. Your blood pressure rises to accommodate the need to get blood, oxygen, and other support to all parts of your body that need help *now*; however, if acute stress goes on too long, irritability and anxiety may occur, as well as other health risks. Learning techniques that enhance your ability to cope and effectively deal with these acute situations are essential (see Chapter 10: Wellness and Mindfulness).

Some people live in a state of episodic acute stress, or mini-disasters. This persistent state of tension involves taking on too much—putting "too much on your plate" and never taking anything off it. Some examples are feeling an overwhelming sense of responsibility for family, friends, or work colleagues, sometimes taking on their problems. In a constant state of irritation, bodies react to ongoing worry and anxiety. People in this state tend to put others first, limiting time to care for themselves and failing to learn or use good coping skills. Our system responds to ongoing stressors, continuing to keep the body at high alert, ready to fight or flee. Heart rates and blood pressure increase—a normal and necessary response to immediate problems. But if you keep problems and crises going and fail to properly manage them, these surges, over time, can cause serious health problems, such as heart disease, gut problems, and depression. In an effort to deal with the ongoing issues, some individuals take on negative or unhealthy coping mechanisms, like eating or drinking too much, staying home, isolating from family and friends, or even giving up activities that made them happy.

Chronic stress involves dealing with ongoing and unresolved conflicts, dysfunctional relationships, and social issues that never get fixed or handled appropriately. The stressors may also include situations in which someone has, or perceives to have, no control over his/her life and circumstances. This type of stress takes its toll, bringing with it ongoing and potentially long-term mental and physical health issues.

Building complete understanding and awareness around stress involves looking at how stressors and the resulting behaviors can trigger an improved reaction, using appropriate coping mechanisms, and training yourself to respond more efficiently and effectively. You can get mentally fit and become stronger and better by learning how to take on, or deal with, stress productively. To illustrate that concept, Florida State University, College of Medicine (https://med.fsu.edu) suggests three other classifications or types of stress: toxic stress, tolerable stress, and positive stress. First, think about toxic stress as the bad apple in the orchard. Only a few rotten apples can give the whole orchard a bad reputation. Toxic stress, the most harmful, is caused by repeated and ongoing stress without the benefit of support, protection, or effective coping mechanisms. This ongoing condition overwhelms the system, causing unhealthy biological and psychological responses to threatening experiences (stressors). Additionally, this type of stress experience can bring about long-term problems, making one feel overwhelmed and unable to judge their abilities to effectively control and deal with troubling situations.

Tolerable stressors involve troubling events, significant personal frustrations, as well as serious injuries, a death in the family, and even a natural disaster; however, what makes this stress tolerable is an established support system and a *sense of control*. This system was prepared. It was ready. It was quickly able to alert and bring forth positive coping mechanisms, establishing control over the situation early on. It doesn't mean there are no issues or struggles, but because of this capability, the stress takes less of a physical and mental health toll, and people are able to move forward more quickly and effectively.

Finally, positive stress is the *productive* response to a brief or mildly troubling situation, easily dealt with using pre-existing and attentive support systems, effective coping skills, and the ability to incorporate past successes into the current situation and environment. Understanding the potential for a positive response is key. Stressors, the stress response, and supporting systems work effectively by first keeping us alive, then allowing adaptation, and finally, nurturing growth and revealing how to use these situations to build better more resilient systems.

Rethinking Stress: Can it Be Beneficial?

Do we need stress? Is it useful, even necessary, to build resilience and make us stronger? Think about it using the idea of systems. As mentioned, like the autonomic nervous system, we have built-in structures throughout our body to keep us in balance and alive and to help us deal with or manage situations that threaten or even damage us; however, to work—or to work well—these systems have to be engaged; they need to be strained to get the most out of them. Dr. Serge Campeau has studied "stress-resilience" and "stress habituation," letting us know we can and do *use* stress, or stressful situations, to actually become better and stronger. It is possible not only to handle or manage stress but actually *use* daily hassles, hardships, or even traumatic experiences to build resilience and encourage our potential to become stronger and grow as a result of such events.[1,2]

Resilience

What you can become depends upon what you can overcome.
—Anthony Douglas Williams

Resilience, defined by *Merriam-Webster*, is:

1. The capability of a strained body to recover its size and shape after deformation caused especially by compressive stress.
2. An ability to recover from or adjust easily to misfortune or change.

Dr. Rachel Yehuda, director of the Traumatic Stress Studies Division at the Mount Sinai School of Medicine, studying how trauma and resilience cross generations, defined resilience as "the process of adapting well in the face of adversity or trauma." I like her concept of adapting well. Taken from a psychological perspective, resilience is the mental and emotional capability to cope with troubling, critical events, including trauma, and respond, recover, and rebound quickly. It is a skillset that allows our mental processes and behaviors to adapt well, and it protects us from the potentially negative effects brought on by stressful events. In promoting the idea and ability to become

---

[1] Radley, Jason, David Morilak, Victor Viau, and Serge Campeau. "Chronic Stress and Brain Plasticity: Mechanisms Underlying Adaptive and Maladaptive Changes and Implications for Stress-related CNS Disorders." *Neuroscience and Biobehavioral Reviews, 58,* 2015. 79–91.

[2] Baratta, Michael V., Christina M. Zarza, Devan M. Gomez, Serge Campeau, Linda R. Watkins, and Steven F. Maier. "Selective Activation of Dorsal Raphe Nucleus-projecting Neurons in the Ventral Medial Prefrontal Cortex by Controllable Stress." *The European Journal of Neuroscience, 30(6),* 2009. 1111–1116.

stronger, or even grow after trauma, I think of resilience as engaging in the process well, thus allowing you to bounce back and become *better*.

It is important to remember that resilience, like other responses, doesn't just happen. It needs to be triggered; there needs to be a stressor that engages systems to respond and react. I use the example of making my muscles stronger. I can't simply sit around and wish them to be stronger. I have to provide a stressor, which is weight training, to push their ability and capacity and work them out, and it is then that they respond by becoming bigger and stronger. Sometimes when pushing to improve muscle strength, it hurts. You can even get injured if you push too much or workout too hard; however, you learn from those mistakes and injuries. Those teachable moments allow you to assess what works and what doesn't and figure out how to move forward. Your system works with you as you gain knowledge about how far you can, or should, push yourself to get the best results and reduce the risk of injury. It may be that you need to slow down, adapt, and adjust or seek help from an expert to improve and get the best results.[3]

Our immune system is another good example of positive stress. That system doesn't just independently make antibodies or figure out how to destroy pathogens, including viruses and bacteria. It needs to be threatened and challenged to do so. When we encounter a germ or virus, the immune system becomes engaged then responds. The system reacts, and if the threat is new, the system may falter a bit. You may not feel well for a time, perhaps even get sicker before you get better, but you can rally and eventually heal. The system has recognized the infection and keeps track of its elements so the next time you get exposed to that germ, it can respond more quickly and either you do not get sick or you have a milder case. If a system(s) is already compromised or if there are conditions that overwhelm it, infections

---

[3]   Ashokan, Archana, Meenalochani Sivasubramanian, and Rupshi Mitra. "Seeding Stress Resilience through Inoculation." *Neural Plasticity,* 2016. 4928081–6.

can bring about significantly troubling or negative results, no matter the response; however, in general, this is basically how immunizations work. Your immune system is provided a "taste" of the pathogen or infection, allowing it to recognize it then respond and react appropriately in the future.

Challenges and struggles can be like immunizations: tolerable, perhaps even positive stresses to enhance our psychological and emotional systems.[4,5] It is a way to practice and build resilience. When faced with adversity, how we learn and the responses and strategies we use to tackle smaller problems strengthen our system so we can handle not only day-to-day frustrations better, but this preparation gets us ready to deal with the bigger, more dreaded problems. It is absolutely necessary to effectively learn how to deal with and *use* minor, less challenging problems to grow and become tougher. View them as opportunities, as positive stressors that strengthen and prepare our systems to respond more quickly and more forcefully when major life events occur. No one gets away from disappointments and struggles. You didn't get the grade you wanted or thought you deserved; you had an argument with a spouse or work colleague; you got a parking ticket, a flat tire, or you missed the bus—to name a few of life's daily distresses. When these things happen, I let myself and others spend a little time complaining, getting angry and frustrated. That is natural and actually kind of necessary. But then, I remind myself to take daily adversities and *use* them to gain perspective, to become stronger physically, mentally, and emotionally.

After studying hundreds of success narratives and accounts—including those of historical figures, entertainers, entrepreneurs, ath-

---

[4]   Radley, Jason, David Morilak, Victor Viau, and Serge Campeau. "Chronic Stress and Brain Plasticity: Mechanisms Underlying Adaptive and Maladaptive Changes and Implications for Stress-related CNS Disorders." *Neuroscience and Biobehavioral Reviews, 58*, 2015. 79–91.

[5]   Ashokan, Archana, Meenalochani Sivasubramanian, and Rupshi Mitra. "Seeding Stress Resilience through Inoculation." *Neural Plasticity,* 2016. 4928081–6.

letes, medical and nursing professionals, business professionals, veterans, and public and private figures in all domains and disciplines—it became apparent that each one of them had a story, usually several stories about bleak, hard, distressing times, as well as terrible, frustrating defeats. Very honest and transparent about their failures and mistakes, it was clear that over time, they used these adversities and downfalls as driving forces to move forward. It did not happen overnight, but over time, they recognized these hardships and failures as distinct opportunities to learn from and improve upon. These events were not separate from their success; they were foundational and instrumental in achieving ultimate accomplishments. They were an unwelcome but necessary part of the process. They saw past the mistake and problem and pushed themselves.

Let's be clear: when you test or challenge yourself, it is not fun and you won't always win. More often than not, you will fall short of your goal or fail, but winners use failures and disappointments as extreme motivation. Personally, I have had more doors closed on me than opened. Some slammed shut. It hurts. I get angry and scared, no question. But when I calmed down, took time to think about it and talked it over with a trusted friend, mentor or therapist, I learned something from each one of my defeats, obstacles, and disappointments. It starts by me taking personal responsibility then stepping back, taking stock, and assessing the problem or situation. Was there something I could do or could have done better? What information or data am I missing? What help or insight do I need to move forward? Do I need to go in a different direction or with someone else? These defeats and setbacks ultimately motivated and revealed to me *how* to get it right next time. They showed me who I was but even more importantly, who I could grow to be.

Take a minute. Think of something in your life that caused you pain, frustration, and fear. How did you deal with it? What did you learn from the situation? Did you use it to improve and become stronger? How? Be precise in your answers. I specifically ask these questions because I want this book to make you think and continually remind you of how strong you are and what you have accomplished. To focus on what you can control, what you can do or need to do to get it right. To remind you, *you got this!*

What Brain Science Tells Us: Take Control

Dr. Steven Maier, distinguished professor and director of the Center for Neuroscience at the University of Colorado, Boulder, studies stress and what can accommodate or bring forth better results during and after such situations. His research revealed that the experience of *controllability*—whether or not a person or animal experiences control over a stressful situation—can make a positive difference. Dr. Maier's research discovered even the *perception of control* can promote better outcomes brought about by a stressor.[6] Additionally, a stressful situation in which a person can gain, or take over control, can also influence the impact of future challenging experiences, reducing negative effects brought forth by such situations.[7] In other words, the system is triggered when one encounters stressful experiences or conditions. If a stressful condition is arranged so the animal or person has or takes control, that experience becomes less difficult, less stressful. More importantly, the effect of controllability, taking or gaining control over a challenging, even traumatic situation, can protect against future effects from stress, sometimes called *stress inoculation*. This term and this type of cognitive behavioral therapy was devised by Dr. Donald Meichenbaum (see sidebar).

We are just beginning to understand this concept and exactly what is happening in the brain. Research conducted by neuroscientists like

---

[6] Maier, Steven F., and Martin E. P. Seligman. "Learned Helplessness at Fifty: Insights from Neuroscience." *Psychological Review, 123(4)*, 2016. 349–67.

[7] Maier, Steven F. "Behavioral Control Blunts Reactions to Contemporaneous and Future Adverse Events: Medial Prefrontal Cortex Plasticity and a Corticostriatal Network." *Neurobiology of Stress, 1(C)*, 2015. 12–22.

Drs. Serge Campeau and Steven Maier reveal that, for some reason, people can undergo very stressful situations or experiences, but their *perception* involving that event can change, significantly influencing later behaviors. Specifically, Dr. Campeau shared with me that "research is showing that when people have a perception of control after a traumatic experience, it may lead to very different outcomes when compared to a person who sees or identifies the situation as uncontrollable."

So, the degree that one is given or otherwise perceives some level of control after troubling events can have a long-lasting effect, and that, in and of itself, will impact how they may view, interpret, and respond to current and future stressful experiences.

Habituation of Behaviors and the Response to Stress

Dr. Serge Campeau, professor of psychology and neuroscience at the University of Colorado, Boulder, specifically studies the habituation of stressors and calls this *stress adaptation*. Habituation from a psychological perspective means there is a decreased response to a stimulus, in this case a stressor, after repeated presentations of that stressor. For example, you get a new ringtone on your phone that at first draws your attention. It can even be distracting. But over time, you become so familiar to this sound you adapt, paying less and less attention to it. Your response to the sound is lessened, so it doesn't trigger you. That diminished response is referred to as *habituation*. Dr. Campeau's initial research shows if you allow an animal to habituate to a stressor, their physical responses can also decrease, at a later time, to different stressors. Therefore, the impact or importance of learning *how* to deal, how to adapt to a troubling situation, is essential. The way his research team studies this is by using low tone noise with rats. It is not painful, and they actually found after two weeks the animals get so used to the noise they just go to sleep when exposed to it. They learned and effectively dealt with the stressor, and this response allows them to adjust well with entirely different stressful situations. Therefore, Dr. Campeau hypothesizes that there is an idea that at some point, their past has helped them deal with the situation successfully and for one reason or another that protects them during later situations.

Dr. Campeau and his team are still not completely clear *how* habituation happens. He questions if there are changes at the cellular level and if so, what are those changes? What is the exact mechanism? More importantly, how do these—or how can these—changes influence future behaviors and support care and interventions for anxiety and phobia disorders, such as exposure therapy and desensitization treatment.[8]

Habituation as a learned ability—obtaining or increasing control over challenging situations—has gained a lot of traction in developing and supporting strengths-based rehabilitation programs like metahabilitation (see Part Three). If you bar or reduce exposure to stressors, strong positive responses may be weakened. Protecting people from environmental microbes (germs) by overuse of sanitizers and antibiotics has reduced the ability of our immune system, our own immunity, to develop fully and properly, causing a rise in the incidence of allergies and immune deficiencies noted in Western societies. Therefore, attempting to view stress and use stressors as growth-enhancing, looking at what one can do and taking as much control over troubling, even traumatic experiences, is a very promising and sensible approach. It helps one handle or manage such events and, over time, find power and grow as a result of them. Further research supporting these actions is being conducted and will hopefully reveal more information as to why these behaviors and mindsets actually reduce, even prevent, troubles associated with or involved in the aftermath of trauma.

Stress Inoculation and Stress Inoculation Training (SIT)

SIT is a type of cognitive behavioral therapy (CBT) initially developed in the 1980s by psychologist Dr. Donald Meichenbaum. Basically, the focus of the term, process, and therapy is helping people cope and deal with stress effectively and efficiently. This method of psychotherapy emphasizes the necessity of advanced preparation, stress immunizing individuals, helping them to handle and deal successfully with stressors and stress in a resourceful manner to bring forth minimal distress and negative effects.

Conclusion

Looking at the potentially productive effects of stress, especially after trauma, persuading survivors and their families that they have and can take control over aspects of the recovery process, then getting them to believe it is *the* game changer. Research suggests that a combination of recognizing and taking control and using more minor situations to train and support capacity for future adaptation and resilience could be more effective. This two-pronged approach to habituate *and* promote control over one's circumstances may be the best tactic in reducing the risk, preventing damage, and increasing stress resistance and resilience.

Finally, it is necessary to acknowledge when dealing with significant trauma that one clearly does not do this alone. That is actually unwise. To bring about a productive outcome, there needs to be a collaboration with the survivor, family, therapists, and clinicians, keeping in mind that the survivor is the focus. They need to be asked about their expectations, desires, and how they see themselves moving forward. This engagement clarifies and supports the survivor's motivation and helps them with accountability and taking control of their situation. The therapeutic team is the support that informs and guides them forward. Over time, I learned I needed to ask better questions when working with survivors. What are they thinking? What did/do they want? What are their biggest fears and worries? How did they get through troubling, tough times in the past? These are just some inquiries I now understand as essential and informative for me, the survivors, and their support system to discuss and incorporate into their ongoing care. It is not my survival story; it is theirs. My work is to allow them control over their journey, reminding them: *you got this*.

Chapter Contributor
Serge Campeau PhD
Professor; Psychology and Neuroscience
University of Colorado, Boulder

CHAPTER 4

HAPPINESS AND GRATITUDE

Between stimulus and response there is a space. In that space is our power to choose our response. In our response lies our growth and our freedom.
—Viktor Frankl

E veryone wants to find happiness and joy in life, but how do you get it, and how do you keep it? Is happiness a choice, a freedom? Can you make yourself happier? Is it your goal to be happy all the time? Exactly how much influence do you have over your own happiness?

Introduction

Aristotle reminds us that "happiness depends on ourselves," and that it is not pleasure but, rather, the joy we feel when growing to our full potential, including our physical and mental well-being. It is challenging to find an accurate working definition of happiness. One strategy stated by Dr. Sharon Furtak, associate professor of psychology at Sacramento State University, is to start with terms that are thought to contribute to happiness and are more clearly defined, such as optimism, flow, and well-being.

This chapter provides insights, ideas, and research regarding these important questions and offers useful information to support your ability, capacity, and understanding of how you can choose your response, to support well-being and happiness.

The expressed intent of this book is to provide information on productive survival practices and continually remind you of your strength and what builds resilience, even growth, in the aftermath of challenges and traumas. There are behaviors and mindsets in your control that help you effectively deal with life's trials and troubling events. We are naturally wired to recognize emotionally negative events very quickly and effectively; however, within our control is also the ability to counteract these associations and focus on the positive. As a result, we can gain a sense of happiness and joy and are then able, as the Dalai Lama and Desmond Tutu state in *The Book of Joy*,[9] to transform it from an ephemeral or temporary state into an enduring trait or habit that becomes a lasting way of being. Acquiring abilities and becoming competent—even exceptional—in certain areas of life, using fine-tuned and reliable skills, is never an accident. It is intentional, the result of sincere effort and a pattern of making wise choices when faced with many alternatives. It is useful to view happiness in this manner—as an informed choice and a learned skill. It is an important planned act that makes you feel good but also improves your overall personal and professional health and wellness. If you are happier, you tend to have better relationships, more stable marriages, higher incomes, are more creative, and have the capability to better fight off illness because you have stronger immune systems.[10]

There are individual differences in well-being and happiness that are influenced by genetics; however, recent research also reveals that you have and can apply significant influence and control over your own happiness. People who chose to take the time and made the effort to engage in positive intentional activities, such as thinking gratefully, optimistically, and mindfully, over time became significantly happier.[11] In the midst of and in the aftermath of challenges and traumatic situations, it is especially helpful to be reminded of this power and your ability to choose and build constructive habits specifically happiness and joy.

Happiness Set Point

Dr. Sonja Lyubomirsky, distinguished professor of psychology at University of California, Riverside, developed the notion of a genetic set point for happiness. Her work and research suggests you are born with a range of happiness that you fall into most of the time. After experiencing really good or positive events, you usually return to your happiness set point. Studying identical twins—individuals with effectively the exact genome or genetic makeup—revealed approximately 50 percent of the differences identified in our level of happiness is set, or determined, by our genes. This is referred to as your *genetic set point* or *genetic set range*. If 50 percent of your happiness is based on genetics, then what accounts for the other half? Your environment, your income, social status, age, and even where you live accounts for 10 percent of the differences in your happiness, leaving another 40 percent unaccounted for. This unaccounted area is the space to engage conscious and intentional activities—actions and behaviors that *you* choose on a regular basis and that create rituals and habits to increase and sustain your happiness.

When considering intentional activities, remember that variety is the spice of life. It is suggested that you pick and engage in an activity you enjoy on a daily basis; and to get the most out of that activity and enhance your happiness, change it up a bit. Take different routes on your daily walk, run, or bike ride. Vary part of your regular

---

[11] Sin, Nancy L., and Sonja Lyubomirsky. "Enhancing well-being and alleviating depressive symptoms with positive psychology interventions: A practice-friendly meta-analysis." *Journal of Clinical Psychology, 65(5),* 2009. 467–487.

or daily "happiness" routine. Socialize, pray, knit, sew, join a book club, or play cards or chess with a variety of people. Be diverse with your friends and activities. Think about actions that brought you happiness in the past and re-engage and return to those. Take control, incorporate the practice of gratitude, and remember that good, deliberate choices bring the best results. One of the great benefits of this is that the more you practice these happiness-evoking skills, the less effort they take. In time, they become automatic and routine.

Your Brain Responds to Being Happy!

You have about one hundred chemicals in your brain called neurotransmitters. These chemicals help to connect areas of your brain, transmit messages, and modulate or balance your mood. Dopamine and endorphins are two hard-working, feel-good brain chemicals associated with pleasure, happiness, and triggering positive feelings. Seeking out and engaging in experiences that bring you pleasure explicitly increase dopamine in the brain, resulting in what we perceive as happiness. Think about the last time you ate your favorite food. Did you feel a sense of pleasure and happiness? Also consider activities like exercise and meditation. These pursuits reduce feelings of pain and boost pleasure, generating a sense of calmness, a positive state of mind and feelings of well-being by releasing endorphins and dopamine.

Why Study Happiness?

In almost every culture and society, people consider the pursuit of happiness a priority and a valued goal. This is one of the most relevant and important dimensions of the human experience, bringing numerous benefits to individuals, communities, and societies. Therefore, attention must be directed to study and apply this behavior.[12] Gaining knowledge regarding the experience of happiness and lasting joy is important because of three outcomes: there are clear

---

[12]   Lyubomirsky, Sonja. "Why Are Some People Happier Than Others?" *American Psychologist, 56(3)*, 2001. 239-249.

and specific benefits to those behaviors; there are direct and positive steps and interventions allowing one to achieve this state of mind and being; and science has revealed that incorporating these practices on a regular basis can help one effectively cope with and overcome challenges and adversity. Happiness *can* make you stronger and more resilient. Therefore, these aspects of human behavior must be studied to gain further information regarding their positive influence on our overall health and wellness, as well as to clearly determine how one can engage in practices that directly influence happiness levels and build resilience to support healthy lifestyles.

Why Focus on the Positive?

For many years, research tended to focus on the negative or adverse effects of physical and psychological problems. We have depression scales, anxiety scales, and pain scales. We have spent a significant amount of time on how to help struggling individuals instead of investigating what makes people, organizations, and communities stronger, happier, and more resilient and discovering exactly how that happens. It's vital that people identify their level of happiness and joy and pinpoint environmental factors and activities that support the ability to maintain those traits, especially in ways that help them overcome life's challenges and adversity. To encourage and support these behaviors brings control and allows you to focus on what you can do in achieving and sustaining happiness. Thankfully, over the last several years, there has been a more balanced commitment to include studies on positive and constructive behaviors—like happiness and posttraumatic growth—guiding interventions that support these aspects of health and wellness.[13,14] Scientists have been able to measure happiness

---

[13] Fordyce, Michael W. "Development of a program to increase personal happiness." *Journal of Counseling Psychology, 24(6),* 1977. 511–521.

[14] Seligman, Martin E. P., Tracy A. Steen, Nansook Park, and Christopher Peterson. "Positive psychology progress: Empirical validation of interven-

ANATOMY OF A SURVIVOR

by paying attention to exactly how it works, and identifying specific behaviors and interventions that positively influence levels of happiness, benefiting individuals, families, and society at large.

Growth Mindset

Several years ago, Dr. Carol Dweck and colleagues became curious about students' attitudes regarding success and failure. They noticed that some students rebounded and adapted after struggles and disappointments rather quickly, while others seemed devastated by even the smallest setbacks. After studying the behavior of thousands of children, Dr. Dweck came to some very interesting conclusions, coining the terms *fixed mindset* and *growth mindset* to describe the underlying opinions people held regarding their learning and intelligence. Her research found that belief in oneself plays a major role in outcomes. Students who learn to believe in themselves and their ability to become smarter do just that. More importantly, they understood the *effort* they put forth made the difference. A growth mindset occurred when students understood that putting more time and energy into their work led to better outcomes and higher achievements.

How Is the Brain Involved?

The brain is intricately involved in this process and activity. Advances in neuroscience revealed information on the brain's plasticity, its ability to be "flexible" and continually change and adapt. Connections between neurons (brain cells) can be newly formed and become stronger with experience and practice. Connections not being used can break and fade away. Actions and behaviors like those supporting good health and positive outlooks—using productive strategies to accomplish tasks, creativity, and good problem-solving techniques—

---

tions." *American Psychologist, 60,* 2005. 410–421.

build new connections and strengthen existing connections to help with brain potential and growth.

Additional research reveals a direct connection between personal beliefs, behaviors, and outcomes. If you *believe* in the ability of your brain to heal, change, and become stronger, you behave differently. This belief directly affects motivation and action. So, one might wonder, can you change a mindset? If so, how can you develop a growth mindset? Great news. Science tells us you can influence growth mindsets—even change from a fixed to a growth one—but it requires you to act, first by believing it can happen. If you have confidence in what neuroscience has discovered, consider this: your brain responds to the commands you give it and the consistent, repetitive efforts you take, even in the face of failure, allows it to perform better. This mindset, this practice, leads to increased drive, dedication, resilience, and positive achievement, hallmarks of a growth mindset.

Think about it. Do you remember a time when you clearly created your own productive reality or truth? What did you do to generate that positive outcome or reality? Be precise. What thoughts did you hold? What actions did you take? Consider past successes and recognize the connections between positive, courageous personal beliefs and effort, drive, and outcome. *You got this.*

Although there is no exact formula or timeline and the process is not the same for everyone, there are some well-researched approaches and behaviors that support and allow you to increase your psychological and mental fitness and belief in yourself. Devising clear and effective strategies, based on past successes as you move forward in life, is key.

Support Your Mental Fitness by Developing a Growth Mindset

Supporting your capacity to grow in the aftermath of trauma is the clear focus of this book. All too often therapeutic goals in the aftermath of challenges and trauma concentrate on ridding people of their problems instead of *using* them as important teachable moments. People learn how to effectively adapt, implement strategies, and become stronger as a direct result of them. This shift in attention and focus to a *growth* mindset, as compared to a *fixed* mindset, changes one's attitude regarding failure, setbacks, and rebounding abilities and helps one pursue and successfully develop what Desmond Tutu and the Dalai Lama call "mental immunity" and what I call "mental fitness." The next section offers suggestions to do just that.

Strategy: A Plan of Action Designed to Achieve a Major Goal

The difference between a dream and a goal is an action plan.
—Dr. Phil McGraw

People approach every life situation with a plan, a strategy directing and guiding them toward a desired outcome. You might have a strategy on how to get a job, speak with your teenager or significant other, deal with an angry boss, lose weight or start a physical activity program, or for any number of life situations. Developing strategies around these situations can help you when facing more significant experiences, such as a cancer diagnosis and treatment, COVID-19 diagnosis and issues, job loss, a divorce, or loss of a child or family member. The "how to"—building strategies and implementing systems to guide you through disappointments, traumas, and crises—is critical. Promoting happiness has clearly been identified as one of the strategies used to reinforce your general well-being, as well as providing support during challenging and tough times.

As a clinician and consultant, I ask simple but informative questions regarding prior activities that were enjoyable and brought success. You can ask them of yourself as well. My first question to both individuals and organizations is always about prior effective actions:

Question 1: What worked? Specifically identify activities used in the past that made you or your organization stronger.

Question 2: What skills are required? What skills have you developed around those activities that ensure success?

Question 3: Clarify motivation and drive. What motivates engagement in these self-identified behaviors and activities that promote your happiness, feelings of joy, and personal contentment?

I ask these questions because they are fundamental to success, and those questioned are the only ones with accurate answers. It is critical for you to recognize and use strategies and processes that *worked* for you, especially before trying new things. I want to set people and organizations up for success and to gain control by, first and foremost, identifying past healthy, effective behaviors that you used, and spend time refining them. Then I suggest you consider adding one new activity and skill to your toolbox for future use. It might surprise you that there is significant scientific support for certain practices and strategies that you used in the past. As you continue reading, you will understand why those behaviors worked.

I use running and other physical activities on a daily basis as a strategy to help me find joy, support my happiness, and reduce my stress. I made it a habit, a ritual, so if I miss a day, I feel odd, or off, and very uncomfortable. If I allow myself to get too far from these routines and activities, I risk losing my mental, spiritual, and physical edge and stability, so I work to maintain a schedule. I obviously have adapted running as an important and helpful activity but there are many others – what do you like to do? Choose an activity that you enjoy and purposefully plan to include it in your schedule. Pick a specific time of day or week that you know works for you—and schedule time to volunteer, bike, hike, knit, paint, sleep, pray, call a friend or whatever combination of behaviors works for you and increases the good neurotransmitters and your happiness. Sometimes you may want to go it alone and have time to yourself while other times it is helpful to engage friends in the activity. It is essential to treat these behaviors with the strict discipline you use in taking medicine or vitamins, getting to work, or meeting other deadlines. These are important and necessary behaviors, so treat them as such. I do not work my running or walking around other daily activities; it *is* a daily activity. I schedule other tasks around my running. For me, it works best first thing in the morning. What works for you?

Friendships also play an essential and supportive role in our health, well-being, and happiness.[15,16] I have been running and walking daily for over thirty years, but I can still find excuses not to run as far or fast on my own, so I built in a support system: I meet friends. Critical to my success is running with different friends and taking different routes, depending on the day, but I get it done. This is not a privilege; it is a necessity. Since I have given myself the permission—the gift—to support my own happiness and overall wellness, I encourage others to do so as well. Also, if I recommend certain behaviors and strategies to others, I must be willing to do them myself. There are actually some fairly easy steps you can take to build and maintain a level of happiness and contentment. The following information provides direct and specific suggestions based on what brain and happiness science tells us works.

[15] Demir, Melikşah, and Ingrid Davidson. "Toward a Better Understanding of the Relationship Between Friendship and Happiness: Perceived Responses to Capitalization Attempts, Feelings of Mattering, and Satisfaction of Basic Psychological Needs in Same-Sex Best Friendships as Predictors of Happiness." *Journal of Happiness Studies, 14(2),* 2012. 525–550.

[16] Demir, Melikşah, Alexandra Tyra, and Ayça Özen-Çıplak. "Be There For Me and I Will Be There For You: Friendship Maintenance Mediates the Relationship Between Capitalization and Happiness." *Journal of Happiness Studies, 20(2),* 2018. 449–469.

It is helpful when clinicians and therapists encourage their clients to regularly practice and keep a record to document the positive strategies they incorporate into their everyday lives. It helps them turn these strategies into habits. It is also suggested that healthcare professionals integrate positive psychology techniques into their *own* life to assist with their clinical work and personal well-being. I not only consider this fundamental to my health and wellness, but if I am asking patients, clients, and my children to adopt and incorporate positive psychological interventions (PPIs) and practices that promote healthy minds and bodies, I must do so as well.

The constitution only guarantees the American people the right to pursue happiness. You have to catch it yourself.
—Benjamin Franklin

What can you do to "catch happiness" and find joy in your life? By staying on top of your mental health and supporting your mental fitness. Here is how. It is often assumed that finding joy in life, or being happy, is caused by a natural disposition or temperament. Although this idea may have some merit, more recent research reveals that people have a space in which to influence and cultivate a happy disposition by faithfully practicing positive activities. Let me remind you to exercise control over situations by focusing on what you can do and adapting and adjusting to troubling situations quickly and effectively. Spend less time ruminating on mistakes and shortcomings; instead, use them to productively guide your next best step. Incorporating intentional positive activities, like expressing gratitude and practicing kindness, leads to wellness and happiness. Science has provided direct evidence supporting such behaviors, thus encouraging and adopting positive activities to sustain happiness is an important practice in life.

The next section provides well-researched positive approaches and techniques to habituate and build your mental strength and happiness. Intentional activities aimed at cultivating positive feelings, behaviors, and mindsets—also called *positive psychology interventions* (PPIs), enhance your overall well-being. Dr. Sharon Furtak reminds us that it takes some time and effort at the beginning, but after a while these positive behaviors become natural—almost automatic. Shifts in brain circuits brought about by positive changes allow you to learn new stimulus-response associations. Once established, these strong connections support those habits. Think about some negative habits you have and how hard they are to change. Here, we are leveraging the strength of habits for good practices. Practice makes perfect, so taking the time and making the effort to integrate and practice PPIs, or happiness-boosting strategies, and continuing to engage in these activities over time improves well-being and can even lower depression.[17,18] Also, it seems that a "shotgun" approach, using a variety or multiple PPI activities, is helpful and more effective than engaging in only one activity.[19,20]

Finally, surviving and dealing with my own brush with death caused a change and an adjustment in the manner in which I interact with patients, students, and even my own children. I spend less time telling them exactly what to do, recognizing that my job or role is more as a consultant, providing appropriate information to advise, support, and guide their health and wellness. I listen first, then give the best information I have based on up-to-date research; provide the best treatment options, interventions, and wisdom; then ask them what they want and think they can do. As I inform and guide, I keep things simple and easy, consistently engaging the person in the process and solution. I question them about what they like to do and which activ-

[17]   Seligman, Martin E. P., Tracy A. Steen, Nansook Park, and Christopher Peterson. "Positive psychology progress: Empirical validation of interventions." *American Psychologist, 60,* 2005. 410–421.

[18]   Taylor, Charles T., Sonja Lyubomirsky, and Murray B. Stein. "Upregulating the Positive Affect System in Anxiety and Depression: Outcomes of a Positive Activity Intervention." *Depression and Anxiety, 34(3),* 2017. 267–80.

[19]   Fordyce, Michael W. "Development of a program to increase personal happiness." *Journal of Counseling Psychology, 24(6),* 1977. 511–521.

[20]   Seligman, M. E. P., T. Rashid, and A. C. Parks. (2006). "Positive psychotherapy." *American Psychologist, 61(8),* 2006. 774–788.

ities bring meaning and happiness.[21] Using simple PPIs to increase wellness and support happiness as a lasting way of being in the world is essential. As a reminder, happy people tend to socialize more often and are grateful and optimistic in their behavior and thinking.[22] Other suggestions include meditating, journaling, writing letters expressing gratitude, counting your blessings, performing simple acts of kindness, identifying and cultivating personal strengths, and considering a positive future.[23] Added to those are some fairly easy steps you can take to build and maintain a level of happiness and contentment.

Getting Happy versus Making Yourself Happy

Choice not chance determines your destiny.
—Aristotle

Let me share some fundamental ideas to help and support you. First, take control of the process of being happy. It is essential to realize that you don't get happy, you *make* yourself happy—and that is good news! It takes time, motivation, and effort, but through the use of some relatively simple actions, you can train yourself, your brain, and affect your own happiness. Next, perspectives you take allow you to change how you feel by changing the manner in which you view or think about a situation. Finally, make the process or strategy relatively stress-free. Start by using what worked before, and as you master those skills, consider adopting new ones.

[21] Lyubomirsky, Sonja, and Kristin Layous. "How Do Simple Positive Activities Increase Well-Being?" *Current Directions in Psychological Science: A Journal of the American Psychological Society, 22(1)*, 2013. 57–62.

[22] Lyubomirsky, Sonja. "Why Are Some People Happier Than Others?" *American Psychologist, 56(3)*, 2001. 239–249.

[23] Layous, Kristin, Kate Sweeny, Christina Armenta, Soojung Na, Incheol Choi, and Sonja Lyubomirsky. "The Proximal Experience of Gratitude." *PloS One, 12(7)*, 2017. E0179123.

As you engage in the suggested practices listed below, consider them as prescriptions or medications. They are supported by research, providing the proper dose and frequency to get the best results—the optimal effectiveness. Don't overwhelm yourself. Pick one new thing to do; don't try to do them all, at least not right away.

- To begin, focus on what you *can* control and what *can* be done. This is key.

Identify your signature strengths and behaviors and build on them. These are activities and mindsets you have already put into play, perhaps even refined. It may be your attitude, what you have for breakfast, when you can exercise or socialize, whatever—always start with what works and what you can personally control. If you are doing these positive things already, it means you like them, so continue and spend time getting better and improving them.

Consistently work to build your motivation, supporting your efforts to control, empower, and build happiness. The decision that life is worth living comes from you. What is it that you can hold onto? What will drive you?

For these next activities, pay attention to the dosing and frequency of the behaviors. Keep a journal. Documentation leads to insights and accountability regarding personal effort as you begin these practices. Try to choose the same day and basically the same time to create a habit and discipline around the activities.

- Gratitude and the grateful brain: Once a week

To build the habit and get the best results, choose one day a week to identify and write down three things you are grateful for. Change them up weekly and keep them fresh in your mind. Science reveals you can notice a difference within six weeks.

- Practice acts of kindness: Once a week

Choose one day, preferably the same day each week, and engage in five simple acts of kindness. Again, as with gratitude, mix it up. Call a person, help someone take out the garbage, feed someone's parking meter, smile and say hello to a stranger, hold a door open—simple things. You will make someone feel better, and you will feel better as well.

- Physical activity: Minimum of five days a week, twenty to thirty minutes each day

I call it the E-Pill (exercise pill). Some people do not like the word or idea of exercise, so instead I suggest using the phrase "physical activity," something that causes you to get a little out of breath. Take time and engage in an activity *you* enjoy. Research is clear that being physically active provides better circulation (blood supply) to all areas of your body, including your brain, helps control weight, and brings forth "feel-good" brain chemicals like endorphins and dopamine to keep you happy and to keep your mind and emotions balanced. Additionally, being active reduces your risk for heart disease, type 2 diabetes, dementia, and Alzheimer's disease. Again, change things up a bit by varying your type of exercise, route, distance, and companions.

- Spiritual activity: Daily; once a week on a more formal basis

Practicing some type of spiritual activity helps. A daily short prayer, recitation of a positive intention(s), or a ten-minute meditation is preferable. Some people also appreciate the more formalized weekly ritual of attending religious services and/or practices on a regular basis. Again, this is helpful in providing the mindset to accept happiness and joy into your life. (See Chapter 10: Wellness and Mindfulness for more ideas.)

- Social connections: Create them, sustain them, and strengthen them

Make good, positive, and engaging social connections. They will be lifelines for you to give and receive happiness, providing support in troubling times. Friends and friendship make a difference—stay connected.

- Choose some of your own fun and healthy activities that bring forth and increase positive feelings, thoughts, behaviors, and satisfy *your* emotional needs.

- Finally, try to incorporate *one* new behavior you find interesting or appealing every few months. That opens up new possibilities and allows you to make new friends.

The Basics: Three Simple Ideas about Happiness

1. **Choice:** You have a say in how you handle challenges and build your capacity for happiness. Make brave and positive choices. Always ask yourself: What have I done in the past that has worked? Identify and choose signature activities, mindsets, perspectives, and strategies, and bring them to the forefront to use again.

---

2. **Control:** There are aspects involving your happiness that are under your control. To the best of your ability, exercise control over your mind, thoughts, and attitudes, as well as your environment. Create a mental and/or physical place where healing and happiness can occur.

3. **Modeling the Way:** Teach resilience, gratitude, and grit. Use your actions to show others that you can and do move forward and exactly how that happens. Model behaviors that reveal those abilities, as well as how to grow after trauma. The next generation will appreciate and use what you taught them.

Conclusion

Science has provided direct evidence regarding the practices and principles of happiness and, even more importantly, *how* to achieve and sustain happiness and joy in your life. The good news is much of the capacity and control lies within you; therefore, you no longer need to rely on unsubstantiated information and opinions from self-help books, advertisements, or slick infomercials. A growing body of credible research clearly demonstrates that making relatively simple, positive, and intentional changes to your thoughts and behaviors on a regular basis brings forth constructive habits that can increase your happiness, well-being, and mental fitness. Confucius suggested that life is actually pretty simple, and we are the ones insisting on making it complicated. So, keep it simple and focus on what matters. Don't let yourself be overwhelmed. *You got this!*

Chapter Contributor
Sharon Furtak, PhD.
Associate Professor of Psychology; Sacramento State University

CHAPTER 5

GENETICS AND EPIGENETICS: HOW NURTURE AND NATURE INFLUENCE RESILIENCE AND GROWTH

What Columbine and COVID-19 Revealed about Building Resilience: A Mother-Daughter Story

Mother

I t was a regular day at Columbine High School, but it is a day she remembers, always. Alma was teaching one of her math classes when she heard something—a loud noise. Growing up with a father who hunted, she immediately recognized gunshots. *Weird,* she thought, *what is that about?* A special education teacher was also in the classroom and left to see what the commotion was all about. Just as

Alma was about to move on with her teaching, her colleague ran back into the classroom and yelled, "Get the children out! There is a shooting!" She calmly and quickly moved the children into the hallway and out of the building. Focused on her students, she was worried about them, their safety and survival, but she also knew that when this was over, there would be major, troubling issues to contend with, both personally and professionally. To this day, she is still disheartened that it was students who perpetrated this event. . . so tragic all around.

Alma struggled with that day and the aftermath. Attending multiple funerals of those who were killed at the high school added to her grief and depression. Twelve students and one teacher were murdered, and there were multiple other injuries. The injuries were not only physical; they were deep and emotional—the kind that really never goes away. As I mention in other parts of the book, you don't get over trauma; you eventually, with time, learn how to use it and incorporate it into your life's meaning. Alma did that, but it took time and the help of others.

She remembers being almost numb, not able to function well. She worried about her two daughters. *How were they dealing with this?* And what could she and should she do to help? They used the support of their family and friends. They also sought and received spiritual counseling; but interestingly enough, both Alma and her daughter, Ashley, told me that in retrospect, they really needed more—more specialized counseling to deal with trauma. Both mother and daughter said that if there was one thing they would do differently, it would be to get that expert help.

"We all slept together in the same room for a while." Alma, her husband, Ashley, and Amy. It just felt better for them all. Nighttime is so hard. It is quiet and thinking comes easier; remembering comes easier, too.

Overall, they did the best they could, and with the support of their spiritual community and friends and family, they got through. Grandparents came to stay the first month and again other times during the first year, just to take care of day-to-day events and activities, allowing the family to begin recovering and healing. Alma praises her neighbors and others who came forward, people she didn't know that well, with movie tickets and gift cards for massages and pedicures. She laughs now, having never had a massage before, after she was given that gift, she gets them regularly.

A special memory Alma shared was, "One evening, several days after the event, I was doing dishes, and Ashley just walked up behind me, hugged me, and said, 'What can I do to help you? Is there anything that I can do?'" Alma reflected on that through her tears, "Can you believe this little twelve-year-old child had that insight and empathy?" She remembered how much Ashley took on and to this day, thanks her for that. She is not sure where that strength and sense of responsibility came from, but it was noticeable.

Alma is a runner. But she didn't run for a while. It was a struggle just getting out of bed and engaging with the day. A little while after the shootings, her loving and supportive husband John said to her, "You need to get out of bed and go for a run." At first, she didn't want to budge, but she did. They ran together, and it was so helpful. She said, "Sometimes you just need to get up, get going, and move on."

Interestingly, when interviewing her daughter Ashley on a separate occasion, she told me the same thing. "Sometimes you just need to deal with the situation and move forward." They did—as a family and as a community. It wasn't easy, and it's still painful when she speaks about it, but lessons were learned about the appreciation for life, family, and relationships. She is there to support her daughter now. Ashley, an emergency room physician in Manhattan, is dealing with a lot—and now, Alma is there to help her.

It was later noted that several bombs were set to go off that day at the school, a couple in the cafeteria and some in cars in the parking lot. They never detonated; why is unclear. In speaking with me, Alma cried a bit. Completely understandable, I do the same. It isn't that you haven't dealt with the event or haven't grown from the experience.

Those events leave marks on the memory center of your brain, as well as on your DNA. Like a fractured bone or a scar from a cut, it may be healed, but the remains are the reminder.

Daughter

"There has been a shooting at Columbine, but your mother is OK."

Ashley was taken out of her seventh-grade class. "What do you mean? Where is she?" Ashley, twelve years old at the time, attending a middle school, vividly remembers being taken into the principal's office and told, "There has been a shooting at your mother's school, but she is OK."

That was the beginning of a new life for Ashley. Although she wasn't at Columbine, she, her sister, and her father were significantly affected. Not only were they worried because of their mother, but they felt the community's response to this terrible tragedy as well. They were unable to get away from it. It was on the news constantly. One of the boys, Dylan Klebold, actually lived in a nearby neighborhood.

Ashley clearly recalls thinking, "I was the oldest and immediately felt like I needed to help my mother and especially my younger sister." She stepped up, thinking about the needs of others; it seemed natural. She just knew others were suffering. Not completely sure how to help, she tried, as her age permitted, to be there and be supportive. She is not sure if this is what prompted her desire to be a physician, but it is clear that this life experience provided the empathy and confidence to do so. "No one in my immediate family is a physician or a nurse. How I decided on being a physician, I am not sure."

Finishing with medical school, Ashley was in an interview for a residency program. She intended to be an emergency physician specializing in pediatrics. Sitting in front of a renowned expert in childhood development, he asked what made her decide on this specialty? Almost without thinking, she shared her experience with the Columbine shootings. She actually hadn't planned to; the memory just seemed to come forward. She told him about her mother, a teacher at Columbine High School. Her mother was there, helping save the lives of her students. She shared recollections of what she, her family, and the other children and students in the community dealt with.

"Maybe that is why you chose this field. There was something early on that drew you to medicine and this particular specialty," he said. As Ashley reflected on that interview, she initially thought he was a bit presumptuous. *He had never met me before. How could he say something like that?* she wondered. But now, she understands. He was a well-known child development scientist and researcher. He knew she probably never really made the connection before, but she does now, especially as she looks at her young daughter. What is she going to teach her about the world, resilience, and managing tough times? She learned from her own childhood experience that you can't shield or protect children from everything. Life is going to happen, and there is only so much you can prevent, but you can prepare. Ashley recognizes using lesser problems and disappointments to build resilience and inner strengths is helpful and necessary. She understands it as a wife, mother, and physician as she is dealing with the COVID-19 pandemic in New York City.

I asked her to reflect on the current crisis. Did what she endured in the past train her for this? "Yes, in a way. I am used to pulling off twenty-four-hour shifts. I understand the grind, but I also understand I can play a special role in this situation . . . if I take care of myself." She praises the hospital she is at for immediately and consistently providing essential mental health support to all healthcare and auxiliary personnel. Intervention from the counseling team began almost immediately, and they check in with them regularly.

Reflecting back on Columbine, Ashley does not know if this really resulted from the experience, but she is very empathetic, taking a lot of time with patients and realizing that, "When they come to see me, it's not a good day. They come in because something is wrong, sometimes very wrong, and I understand that and work to be present and as helpful as I can."

It is difficult to separate exactly the role of nurture and nature. After speaking at different times with both women, they saw, felt, and responded with many similar ideas and insights. It is more than likely a balancing act—probably a little bit of both. There are some predispositions to behaviors and characteristics, but there are also environmental triggers or cues for gene expression. This book, especially this chapter emphasizes that what you do, what you control, and your behaviors make a difference in the now and potentially for future generations. The following chapter will help you make more sense of nature—genetics and nurture—*epigenetics,* and your role. Recognize the influences you have to build good coping mechanisms, resilience, and a growth mindset and remember, *you got this!*

Genetics and Epigenetics

We've discovered the secret of life.
—Francis Crick

Why include a chapter on genetics in a book about resilience, grit, and posttraumatic growth? Again, the expressed intention of this book is to empower survivors by reminding them of their natural abilities for survival and growth in the aftermath of trauma, as well as how to build and support these capacities. To strengthen that information, it is necessary to provide evidence supporting suggested actions and behaviors, basically helping to identify the exact anatomy and physiology of a survivor and how they can develop capabilities early on.

Ongoing research fueled by unceasing ambition, amazing discoveries, and advanced technology has brought to light details and answers regarding human capacity, specific behaviors, and personal actions that bring forth optimistic and positive outcomes in the aftermath of trauma, as well as evidence to support why and how they work. It is critical to examine your past successes, assess what behaviors to continue, and identify a few new ideas for what *can be done* to: 1) take control in what seems to be uncontrollable situation(s); 2) understand the science that supports productive behaviors and practices (why what you are doing is a good idea); and finally 3) realize that reinforcing existing growth mindsets and behaviors that improve adaptation, resilience, and growth have profound and very positive consequences for you and possibly your children and their children.

This chapter is intended to cover very basic concepts of genetics so you can understand, on another level, why actions you take and behaviors you adopt have significant immediate consequences and potentially future ones. Having even basic information regarding genetics helps you understand both how you can and do influence your well-being by making informed and productive personal choices. The fundamentals of the two processes that influence genetic expression are explained to help in this understanding. One is the sequence or coding (organizing) of genes. If that process goes awry—if a single gene stops working normally—problems occur, including illness and disease.

The other process does not involve or influence gene sequence. *Epigenetics* recognizes that environmental and behavioral factors contribute to your general state of well-being by silencing or activating your genes. How you behave—your activities and environment—and how you handle joy as well as adversity can all influence your health and wellness in the present and potentially impact future generations.

Let me be clear: there is significantly more to study and know to truly understand genetics and the role it plays in our existence and with our behaviors. But for the purposes of this chapter and the overall content of this book, let me focus on a couple of basic concepts that allow you to understand just how personal choices in the here and now can impact cellular activities and positively influence your skills and abilities, including working through trauma. Starting with a short history and some important definitions of terms, let me explain how genetic information is transmitted from one generation to the next and how characteristics and behaviors get passed on.

Genetics: It Began with Mendel and the Peas

In 1905, William Bateson coined the term "genetics" using the Greek *genno*, meaning "to give birth;" however, Gregor Johann Mendel, a Moravian-Augustinian monk, is considered the founder of the modern science of genetics. A branch of biology that studies heredity, genetics looks at how inherited traits, including physical characteristics, health, and tendencies for specific disease, are transmitted to you by your mother and father.

Mendelian Inheritance

In the nineteenth century, Gregor Mendel became curious about how traits were passed on from one generation to the next. For eight years (1856–1863), he formulated his ideas by hybridization, or plant-breeding experiments, using over 10,000 pea plants that he grew in his monastery's garden. Used because of their easily identifiable traits, Mendel's pea plant experiments revealed that genes come in pairs, inherited as distinct units or factors—one from each parent—and that there are dominant and recessive genes. All this information led to *Mendel's Principles of Heredity*, or *Mendelian Inheritance*. In 1865, he introduced his paper, *Experiments on Plant Hybridization* to the Natural History Society of Brno, and it was published in 1866. Although considered the founder of the modern science of genetics, his research and results were felt to be insignificant and largely ignored at the time. Fortunately, a generation later in 1900, his work was rediscovered by the European botanists Hugo de Vries, Carl Correns, and Erich von Tschermak. Reviewing Mendel's publications and using different plant hybrids, they independently confirmed his findings and were able to expand the awareness of Mendelian laws of inheritance to the scientific world. Cells and chromosomes were now adequately understood, giving Mendel's abstract ideas a more explicit framework or context.

Genes and Chromosomes

Genes, located on chromosomes, are the basic units of inherited information. Genes are segments of deoxyribonucleic acid (DNA) and are involved in the formation and regulation of proteins that guide early development and tissue functions throughout our life-span. There are about 22,000 genes, and most are located in each cell nucleus (center). By way of DNA, genes create proteins to build structures, and those structures determine their specific function. A consequence of altered protein structure is an alteration or change in its function. For example, many proteins interact with and bind to each other through specific regions. These regions have defined shapes derived from the amino acids that make up the protein. These amino acids were defined by the DNA sequence of the gene that encoded each protein. Think of it as a key and a lock. The "key" protein may fit into and unlock the "lock" protein. A change in the DNA sequence can alter the shape of the "key" protein, and as a result, the key no longer fits. If unlocking the "lock" protein is an essential biological function, the defective key can now lead to disease.

An example of a defective key is cystic fibrosis (CF). CF is a hereditary disease that affects the lungs and digestive system as the body produces mucus that is much thicker and more sticky than usual. It is a recessive disease, meaning the defective gene is inherited from *both* parents so both copies of the gene in the child are not functioning correctly. CF is usually diagnosed in young children, and people with the disease tend to have a shorter life-span. This is a rare disease (1,000 cases per year in the US) caused by abnormal DNA sequence in the cystic fibrosis transmembrane conductance regulator (CFTR) gene.

There are 1,700 known mutations associated with CF, which can affect the protein in different ways. Some prevent the normal processing of the protein as it is assembled, some prevent it from moving to where it is needed at the cell surface, and others result in a defectively assembled protein that doesn't function properly. Early intervention is beneficial, so all newborns in the US are screened for the most common CF gene mutations. One of the most common CF protein defects that affect 90 percent of CF patients arises from the deletion of three DNA letters, or bases. In a gene, the protein is encoded by a series of three-letter (base) "words," each representing a specific amino acid, the building blocks of proteins. In this case, one of these "words" in the instructions for making the protein is missing, and as such, the protein that is made is missing an amino acid (at position 508) in its structure. This results in the altered protein getting stuck in one of its processing steps and not making it to the cell surface where it is needed. Of note, this protein missing the single amino acid is able to perform its function reasonably well if it could get to the cell surface, and drugs have been developed to help it reach the cell surface and function better when there.

Chromosomes are structures present in each cell's nucleus (center) and are made up of DNA, histones (a basic protein; keep these in mind, they will come into play later), nonhistone proteins, and ribonucleic acid (RNA). Humans normally have a total of forty-six chromosomes; they get one set of twenty-three from their mother and one set of twenty-three from their father. Of the inherited chromosomes, twenty-two pairs are autosomes (common in both sexes), and you receive one sex chromosome from your mother (X) and one from your father (either X or Y); females are XX and males are XY.

The structure and properties of your body's proteins are determined by the DNA sequence of your genes, providing a code to build the proteins. Each individual has a unique genetic makeup or DNA sequence. This makes them distinct from other individuals, except for identical twins, triplets, or other multiples. A person's genetic makeup plays an important role in their homeostasis (balance), as well as their susceptibility or resistance to illnesses. Their genetic structure determines the range of responses and potentials they have to interact with the environment, bringing about their relative state of health. Questions arise regarding capacity and ability to influence fitness, health, or illness by altering genetics before or after conception. Developments in genetics involving how the environment interplays with *gene expression* after birth provide insight regarding possibilities and abilities to influence how they work.

> Interesting fact: in 1869, DNA was first identified by Swiss researcher Friedrich Miescher. He was studying blood cells and coincidentally noted a new molecule, nuclein/DNA. Recognizing and determining genetic inheritance did not occur until 1943. On February 28, 1953, Cambridge scientists James Watson and Francis Crick determined the structure of DNA was a double helix—a spiral—which led to an understanding of genetic instructions and how they passed from generation to generation. Solving mysteries of science takes a while, but once understood, new ideas are generated and behaviors can be modified to support positive behavior and improve the human condition, such as *epigenetics*.

Human Genome: The Human Genetic Code

Genome is the DNA of an organism and includes the entire collection of genes—the total genetic makeup or complement of a living thing. In an effort to map out the entirety of all human genetic material, its sequence and functioning, The Human Genome Project (HGP) was developed. Beginning in October 1990, the project was completed in April 2003. An international team of scientists from eighteen countries identified the sequence and mapping of all the genes, thus providing the ability to read nature's complete genetic blueprint—what builds a human being.

Epigenetics

Your genetics is not your destiny.
—George M. Church

Think about the genome, the genetic makeup of humans. How much do you think we share? How much are we alike or similar? You might be amazed to discover we are far more alike than we are different. Would it surprise you to know that all human beings are 99.5 percent identical in terms of their genetic makeup? The remaining 0.5 percent holds critical clues and information about health, wellness, and causes of illnesses. Let's look at some exceptions. Although we are extremely similar, identical twins are, well, identical. Their genomes are the same, so it is expected that they have exactly the same physical characteristics, behaviors, even diseases because they have the same chromosomes and DNA sequence; however, over their life-span there may be some differences noted. For example, why does one identical female twin contract breast cancer and the other, her sister, does not? In male identical twins, why would one be diagnosed with prostate cancer and the other not? Is there something other than the gene sequencing that influences health, illnesses, and diseases? Is there something that takes over, that modifies *gene expression*—how genes act?

> Just to be accurate. You might have heard or read that we are 99.9 percent identical in terms of our genetic makeup. That percentage was used after the sequencing of the genome and refers to single base differences. Experts now know that there are insertions and deletions that differ between us and actually account for more DNA differences, so the correct percentage is 99.5 percent.

The genome—the DNA sequence that encodes the genes—is set at the time of conception; however, not all genes are active in all cells at the same time. Even identical twins who share the same genome will show differences in certain epigenetic regions. Environmental cues or triggers can selectively bring about activation (turning on) or inactivation (turning off or silencing) of genes. Rather than altering the genome or the genetic code itself, there is a mechanism called methylation that essentially allows initiation of gene activity. Epigenetics is the term used to describe that activity.

Epi, a Greek prefix meaning "on top of" signifies the feature of genes to be expressed—that is, turned on and/or off based on environmental prompts. Epigenetics specifies the ability of genes to act in a manner that is *in addition to the genetic code itself*, responding and bringing about activity through mechanisms that do not involve changes in underlying DNA sequence but instead are influenced by factors like age, environment, lifestyle, diet, and illness. This affects activation or inactivation of a gene, sometimes an entire chromosome, and occasionally for the life of the cell. Epigenetic modifications bring about changes by using three systems. The first involves DNA methylation, the second influences histone modification, and the third works with non-coding RNA (ncRNA) associated gene silencing. This next section is dense. But it is important to include because, in a very general way, it explains *how* your behaviors can influence activity on a cellular level, revealing a "snapshot" of epigenetics and how that system works, so enjoy it and again, feel free to read it more than once!

How It Works: The Basics of Gene Expression and Modification

First, epigenetics works by attaching a small molecule, a methyl group or tag, to a region of a gene, causing it to turn off or become silent. Methylation is a process best exemplified by Siddhartha Mukherjee in his book, *The GENE: An Intimate History*.[24] He describes using methyl tags to decorate the strands of DNA like charms on a necklace

---

24   Mukherjee, Siddhartha. *The Gene: An Intimate History*, first edition. New York: Scribner, 2016.

or bracelet. Those "charms" influence genes by causing or signaling them to become silent or shut down gene activity.

Secondly, in addition to methyl charms or tags hanging from necklaces or bracelets, another system that has an impact on genes, is histones. They regulate genes by looping or wrapping around chromosomes, affecting gene expression. They cause the chromosome to be condensed, making it smaller so it can fit into the cell nucleus properly. They also influence the transcription or the copying of the DNA into an RNA, which is used to make the protein that genes encode for. Not all areas of chromosomes carry histones, and this aspect determines the areas and which genes are transcribed (copied to RNA) and eventually make proteins. These markers may persist across several generations. "The heritability and stability of these histone marks, and the mechanisms to ensure that the marks appear in the right genes at the right time, are still under investigation," but it does appear that other organisms, such as roundworms, can communicate histone marks across generations.[25]

Finally, a non-coding RNA (ncRNA) is a functional RNA molecule transcribed from DNA but not translated into a protein. Basically, there are three major classes of short non-coding RNAs; microRNAs (miRNAs), short interfering RNAs (siRNAs), and piwi-interacting RNAs (piRNAs). Micro RNAs (miRNAs) work in transcriptional and post transcriptional regulation of gene *expression*. Paring with complementary sequences within the mRNA (messenger RNA) molecules may result in the silencing of a gene *expression*. Additionally, long non-coding RNA (lncRNA) also work in transcriptional and post transcriptional regulation of gene *expression* and can direct changes in the epigenetic states of chromatin (the substance within a chromosome consisting of DNA, RNA and protein).

Presenting this basic genetic and epigenetic information is important and purposeful. It reminds you that you can influence, and exert some control over your life, possibly at the level of your genetics.

---

[25] Ibid. pp 401.

Bottom line: you can't change the arrangement, the sequence of your genes. That is set at conception, but you can still have some effect on how your genes work. Behaviors and activities adopted and environments you choose can make a difference in how your genes express or work in the here and now. My resolve is to support what you can do, the actions you can take, and remind you that you have already developed good coping skills. I want to enhance your awareness and understanding of why taking control and using past successes is a great idea. Also, it is essential to recognize that when you have pushed through and worked through tough stuff, like trauma, and come out better, stronger, and more resilient, you have made a difference; you changed things at a very deep level. This not only positively influences you but possibly your children and your children's children. We can't change the order of genes. That arrangement happened, but we can change the expression of some genes—how they work, by silencing them (turning them off) or turning them on. The content and suggestions in this book clearly present and elaborate on actions you can choose to bring about positive changes in yourself, conceivably at a level as deep as your DNA.

Nature vs. Nurture: Who Rules?

Are you a product of what you were born with or how you were raised? That is the never-ending question. When looking at personalities, characteristics, and behaviors, it is very tough to dismantle and figure out causations of differences and whether they are the result of nature or nurture. I presented a lot of information regarding *nature*, our genetic inheritance creating biological factors that bring about physical and personality traits that do not change regardless of where you were born or how you were raised. *Nurture*, on the other hand, involves the external factors or variables occurring after conception, including one's personal life and the influence of childhood environments, experiences, culture, and family. This section briefly discusses three areas you can influence.

1. Nurture
2. Current behaviors that can influence genes in the here and now
3. Changes in genes that potentially affect future generations

Nurture

This aspect of your life is significant; acknowledging and focusing on external factors you can control is key. These external factors include: efforts you make and behaviors you adopt that influence the here and now; how you adapt and your perception of situations as growth-enhancing; and the development and strengthening of positive coping mechanisms within your control.

When determining outcomes, it is difficult to completely separate genetics/epigenetics from nurture; however, one thing is clear: it is helpful to work toward and maintain your health and wellness. Additionally, research by Dr. Michael Meaney[26,27] shows that the social environment provided in early childhood, along with parental stress or wellness, can cause changes and affect neurodevelopment (how the brain develops), as well as one's overall mental health. Addressing your needs and modeling positive, optimistic, and strength-enhancing activities builds mental and emotional resilience and potentially helps increase resistance to future challenges for you and your children.[28] When they observe you taking on challenges in a positive and productive manner, they feel less stress and will potentially incorporate those traits for themselves in the future.

Current Behaviors Can Influence Gene Expression Now

Epigenetics has shown that turning gene expression off or on is affected by environments, age, and lifestyle. Therefore, taking on challenges and traumas, using suggestions in this book that basically support incorporating past successful resilience and recovery experiences, focusing on what you can control, and perceiving over time what you have gained can likely influence epigenetic mechanisms. It is important to remind you that engaging in stress-reducing, growth-enhancing behaviors is essential to self-care (review Chapter 10: Wellness and Mindfulness). First, because you need it but also because demonstrating those behaviors to others, especially children, can influence their mental health and potentially affect gene expression. Many times, you can't control adversities and trauma, but at some level, you can control the response. This mindset and the utilization of wellness practices have scientific support. Dr. Meaney's research focused on early-life adversities and discovered that these experiences potentially have persistent impacts on gene expression through epigenetic mechanisms.

Changes in Genes that Affect Future Generations

Can environmental messages or triggers convert into a heritable or genetic change? Can they affect the next generation by permanently altering a gene? New and ongoing research is continuously uncovering the role of genetics, especially epigenetics, in a variety of human situations to include resilience and hardiness. These results are hopeful but need further research to more fully understand the genetic mechanisms.[29]

However, if you can pass on stress and the negative aspects associated with it, you can probably pass on the important infrastructures associated with being "unstressed." My ongoing message is one of support – to take care of yourself, keeping the focus on what you can do and what you can control. Science, including genetics, supports self-care and shows why taking on and maintaining a more positive, optimistic outlook and encouraging behaviors that build adapta-

---

[29]   Meaney, Michael J. "Maternal Care, Gene Expression, and the Transmission of Individual Differences in Stress Reactivity Across Generations." *Annual Review of Neuroscience, 24(1)*, 2001. 1161–192.

tion, personal strength, and resilience makes a difference for you and your children.

Advice Regarding Children and Trauma

In the aftermath of traumas, it is necessary to get help and consult with healthcare professionals regarding best practices and care for children. I offer some basic ideas based on information from survivor interviews, research, and experts like clinical psychologist Dr. Erin Skiffer. To begin, when dealing with children, consider their developmental stage and do not try to press your ideas or your approach on them. They may not assess and comprehend situations the way you do. Instead, check in with your children. Recognizing something significant has happened, Dr. Skiffer suggests asking them what they are *thinking* instead of, "How are you?" Do they have any questions or worries? When they ask a question, simply and concisely answer that question as best you can. Then, check in: "Did I answer your question?" They will let you know if there is any confusion. Then very calmly ask, "Do you have other questions?" If they do, again, answer that specific question. If they say no, then reassure them by saying, "If you do, always know you can come to me and ask." If you aren't sure how to answer their question or feel you may not be able to contain your emotions when answering the question, give yourself some time. You might say something like, "What a great question! I'm not sure I know the answer, so how about I gather some information and I'll get back to you on that really soon?"

In speaking to families who experienced traumatic events, like Alma and Ashley, it is a good idea to have your children receive some formal counseling. There will be expected issues like sadness and fears about their future; getting those addressed and attended to helps in the long run. Like Ashley, they may be worried about you (the parent) and are afraid to say anything fearing it will further upset you. They may be confused regarding life in the here and now and are guessing and assuming, unsure of what will happen. Counselors who are experts in this field help children express themselves and make sure they recognize where *their* responsibilities lie and how to deal with any worries, real or imagined, that may arise.

Children need reassurance. They need to know someone is in charge. Get help for yourself so you can help and support your children. It is acceptable to let them see that you struggle at times but are actively seeking help and handling this in a productive manner, thereby modeling good coping skills and showing them that even adults ask for help sometimes. They will be reassured that someone is in control, that their feelings are expected, and that, over time, life will go on and they can and will become stronger.

Be attentive to your child's needs, but remember, there is such a thing as overly reassuring your child. When children begin to excessively seek your reassurance or are not satisfied with your efforts to comfort them, this is a sign, a warning, that they are struggling with issues that may benefit from the support of a professional counselor. They need to develop their own ability to quiet their worries instead of solely relying on your reassurance.

Finally, as children move through developmental stages, also consider that the trauma as they originally understood it may shift and change. As they age, they develop the ability to identify the story of their family's life in more nuanced and sophisticated ways. You may need to return to inviting questions and dialogue. And you may be surprised. They may ask about it out of the blue, when they are in school, or when they are watching a movie that reminds them of their story. Don't be afraid. Recognize it as a part of an ongoing process of recovery, healing, and growth.[30]

---

[30]   Bonanno, George A., and Anthony D. Mancini. "The Human Capacity to Thrive in the Face of Potential Trauma." *Pediatrics (Evanston), 121(2),* 2008. 369–75.

Conclusion

It is tough to dismantle and figure out the basis of our personal differences. Are they a result of nature *or* nurture? Significant questions relating to genetic influences regarding cause, affect, and mechanism of action remain. Can historical memory, like famines, create genetic memory? If children can inherit a parent's trauma, can they inherit their resilience? Can children, grandchildren, even great-grandchildren carry the cellular marks for resilience and hardiness from an earlier generation? Research continues to seek and bring forth answers to those questions. I wanted to offer something to you now, so I went to an expert, Dr. John D. McPherson, a professor of biochemistry and molecular medicine at University of California, Davis. He guided me in understanding this content and offered this insight: "It is safe to say there is good evidence there is persistence of a trait across generations that are not just coded in your DNA. Furthermore, we do not completely understand the mechanisms, but there is evidence revealing the manner in which you personally deal or potentially deal with trauma, can possibly affect your epigenetic profile and may influence the next generation."

Last Words: Shape Your Thinking around Challenges and Trauma by Using Good Generational Advice

Ashley took advice from her mother and recognized good coping skills for dealing with extreme trauma. It quite possibly influenced her choice of specialty in medicine and made a difference in how she dealt with the COVID-19 pandemic. Considering my own family history has led me to question how much I received in terms of grit and resilience. *I got this . . .* or at least some of my relatives did, and remembering or hearing about their stories inspires and guides me.

Recognizing patterns, behaviors, and mindsets in your own family can support you, especially in tough times. Like Ashley and her mother, Alma, take tips and monitor the behavior of those you admire. Talk with your parents and grandparents. Ask someone about a great-grandfather or grandmother, aunt, uncle, cousin, parent, or sibling—people in your family who dealt with and worked through trauma. How did they tackle troubling times and come up bigger and stronger in the face of adversity? Listen to their stories. What moved them forward, kept them going, and gave them strength? You might be very surprised to find out how much strength, grit, and potential for growth is in you.

I asked my amazing Grandma Burns to tell me about her life, my grandfather's life, and their parents' stories. They were born in the late 1800s and early 1900s and experienced a lot of life. Not wanting to forget them and to encourage her to provide details of her life, I gave my grandmother a journal and asked her to write down memories and stories when she thought of them so my children and I would have them to read and reflect upon. I learned a lot and am very glad so much of this family history is documented. She shared a great deal, including that my grandfather lived in an orphanage, how he and her brothers were in WWI, how the family survived the Great Depression, and that her son, my uncle, a Navy pilot during the Korean War, once did a flyover when she and my grandfather lived in Chicago. She died at age ninety-three. That is a self-help book I refer to on a regular basis. Take advantage of your relatives. Use their experiences, stories, and life lessons of survival and resilience and match it with your own grit. And remember, *you got this.*

Chapter Contributors
John Douglas McPherson, PhD
Erin Skiffer, PsyD. Clinical Psychologist

CHAPTER 6

HOPE ENDURES: POSTTRAUMATIC GROWTH— A SHIFT IN FOCUS AFTER CHALLENGES AND TRAUMA

*The world breaks everyone and afterward many
are strong at the broken places.*
—Ernest Hemingway, from *A Farewell to Arms*

A t thirty-two years old, Lane wanted to get out of the cubicle he was working in and explore the world to find himself and plot out the next stage of his life. In January of 2014, taking his passport and backpack, he traveled to southeast Asia. With no set agenda, he did whatever he wanted, whenever he wanted. After three months of traveling in the area, he went to Thailand on a snorkeling expedition. On April 17, 2014, he was taking one last dive. It was dusk. He didn't realize how shallow the water was and, as he told me, "I dove in with all my functions and did not come back out with all my functions." He suffered a head injury and broken neck, causing paralysis at the level of his shoulder and starting "a new life I never asked for..." After finally getting to a hospital, the MRI revealed an injury at C3-C7 (cervical or neck bones). He became a quadriplegic.

When returning to the US, he had surgery and intensive therapy at a special spinal cord injury (SCI) rehabilitation center. The first thirty days consisted of learning the ins and outs of what his new life was going to mean and how to get through each day. Although he was told that what you get back in terms of function and movement happens in six to twenty-four months, he doesn't necessarily believe that. He works hard several hours a day to keep the movement he has, and he has accomplished a lot. He recognizes that making good choices and taking as much control as possible is essential to getting back to having a productive life. "I don't think I will ever accept that I will stay in this chair. With that said, it doesn't mean I can't live a fulfilling life." He has gone skydiving, regularly goes to the gym, returned to school to complete his degree, and is planning to get back into the workforce.

"I don't accept the injury as defining me. It is the hand I was dealt, and I have to make the best of what I have. I can work as hard as I want—maybe I will get everything back, maybe I will get nothing back." For now, his power chair is his legs, and Ziggy, his service dog, helps bring him more independence, as well as companionship. Still wishing things could be different, Lane accepts what has happened but works toward his goal and holds high hope that he will walk again. In terms of lessons, he recognizes that clichés are there for a reason; they are truths. Family matters, you can't buy happiness—and the big one for him—don't sweat the small stuff. "When you are sitting in a wheelchair, you get to observe people, get to know people, get to know yourself . . . I really try to surround myself with individuals who are positive and will bring some optimism and joy into my life; and there are a lot of friends I don't hang out with anymore. Some of it is the natural pathways of life. We all go our separate ways, and some are not positive influences. I don't want them in my life at this point . . . so a big takeaway would be: let life happen and be around people you love."

His Aunt Sally had a hard time and still does. A world-class athlete and accomplished businesswoman, she and Lane would run, swim, and bike together. One of the first people to meet him upon his return to the US, she initially was worried if he would even live through this, then how he would function. Lane is lucky. As he says, "I have been truly blessed with a network of people I have supporting me," including an extended and loving family who had to figure out "how do we support this catastrophic accident in a young man who had an amazing future in front of him? And the really hard question to ask is, 'What is next?'" As Sally told me, "It is not happy to go through this experience, but now, life is *happier*. You see joy in your life, see some happiness, and are staying positive." She pushes him, reminding him that his job is to get out of that wheelchair. "I have been encouraging him to go into his heart, which is the strongest muscle we have," to figure things out, get perspective, and make future plans.

Aunt Sally learned lessons from experiencing this trauma as well. "I learned I take a lot of risk in my life—risk in business, risk in some of the hardest races with the intention of winning—and I have backed up a bit, weighing the risks more. I think this experience has influenced me in terms of my own life and my deep love for my nephew and how I care about him."

Introduction

As stated earlier, trauma, crisis, and challenges are a part of the human condition—some more significant than others. These events change peoples' lives, causing fear and depression because of the disruptions to one's way of living, of being in the world, potentially triggering lasting physical and emotional scars. Survivors can feel cut off, isolated, disconnected, even rejected from a range of activities and lifestyles enjoyed prior to the crisis. Understanding this reality and these issues as important and recognizing my professional obligations, let me shift gears and suggest an additional perspective. It is absolutely necessary to diagnose and address troubling and painful issues brought forth by traumatic events. But we can and should also take a more balanced view, through a hopeful lens and recognize that as unsettling and confusing these events are, they are also, with time and effort, areas in which one can grow, become stronger and generate new and positive mindsets and behaviors.

For decades, scientists have researched trauma and its aftermath, studying survivors' responses, concentrating on the restoration of baseline health. Early investigations focused on the many ways these events led to psychological, emotional and physical problems. Rehabilitation, as a medical model, tended to view trauma, life crisis, and disease largely as the breakdown and malfunction of physical, psychological, and emotional health. Research took a negative focus, looking at the pathology—what went wrong, concentrating more on the problems associated with recovery.[31,32,33,34] That emphasis is understandable and necessary. No question, these events are extremely disturbing and a definite threat to one's physical and emotional well-being. Sadness and depression are common, actually expected, responses. Survivors wish things could be different. Troubling, painful, even dysfunctional patterns of thinking about the event can set in, causing psychological and physical difficulties. The attention to problems associated with dam-

[31]   Substance Abuse and Mental Health Services Administration. "SAMHSA's Concept of Trauma and Guidance for a Trauma-Informed Approach." *HHS Publication, SMA 14–4884.* 2014.

[32]   Ai, Amy L., and Crystal L. Park, C. (2005). "Possibilities of the positive following violence and trauma: Informing the coming decade of research." *Journal of Interpersonal Violence, 20,* 2005. 242–50.

[33]   Mikal-Flynn, Joyce. "MetaHabilitation: How to survive life after trauma." *Nursing Times,* 2012. Web.

[34]   Mikal-Flynn, Joyce. "Posttraumatic growth: Breaking through to recovery." *Nursing, 47(2),* 2017. 48–54.

aging situations is understandable and appropriate, especially when looking at major physical and emotional traumas. Also challenging is clearly defining terms like "health," especially if it is used to describe only a state of being that is useful and active, one that is free from illness or disease. This focus is limiting for both survivors and those providing services. It lacks a complete understanding of notable personal capacities, failing to recognize these events as potentially growth-enhancing, transformative experiences.[35,36,37,38]

Research by Tedeschi and Calhoun (2004) involving trauma and outcomes reveal that there are individuals who do develop long-standing psychological disorders, but fortunately, growth experiences in the aftermath of trauma outnumber the reports of significantly troubling disorders.[39] This by no means is meant to be dismissive or insensitive to the suffering and damage faced by victims, but instead, it is meant to provide encouragement and optimism in terms of what can be accomplished and bring focused care for those who, for a variety of reasons, severely struggle in the aftermath of trauma. Without a doubt, it is necessary to identify the damage and problems brought forth by these experiences; however, research directed toward a fuller understanding, showing the complete picture and possibilities for survivors and their families, is also needed.

Thankfully, in the last several years, research has shifted taking a more even handed approach to the aftermath of trauma and survival.

35 Mikal-Flynn, Joyce. "MetaHabilitation: How to survive life after trauma." *Nursing Times,* 2012. Web.
36 Mikal-Flynn, Joyce. "Posttraumatic growth: Breaking through to recovery." *Nursing, 47(2),* 2017. 48–54.
37 Calhoun, Lawrence G., and Richard D. Tedeschi. *Posttraumatic Growth in Clinical Practice.* New York: Brunner-Routledge, 2013.
38 Jackson, Colleen A. "Posttraumatic growth: Is there evidence for changing practice?" *The Australian Journal of Disaster and Trauma Studies, 2007-1,* 2007. 1–11.
39 Tedeschi, Richard G., and Lawrence G. Calhoun. "Posttraumatic growth: conceptual foundations and empirical evidence." *Psychological Inquiry, 15,* 2004. 1–18.

Inquiries are now directed toward understanding the potential for growth, enhanced by using specific examples gleaned from survivors' documented experiences. This brings forth optimism and specifically aims care and interventions to utilize and incorporate the natural resilient capacity of humans. Trauma and adversity clearly bring forth negative and troubling issues, but they also uncover human potential, including personal control, resilience, strength, and wisdom.[40,41,42,43] Strategic approaches to aftercare need to include and support strengths-based programs and the beneficial aspects of survival and recovery.

Individual, Secondary, and Vicarious Trauma

Individual Trauma

Specific definitions and descriptions of trauma vary according to the underlying illness and damage involved. In general, trauma is a response or a consequence to a terrible event that brings forth harm and detrimental changes to the physical, psychological, and spiritual integrity of a person. In 2014, the Substance Abuse and Mental Health Services Administration[44] defined trauma as an event or situation(s) experienced by an individual as physically or emotionally harmful and potentially life threatening, with potentially lasting adverse effects on the individual's ability to function on all levels and all aspects of life. These experiences are deeply distressing and disturbing to physical, emotional, spiritual, and cognitive abilities, causing social, personal, professional, and economic disruptions. Like Lane, interrupting one's way of living and functioning in the world can make one feel alone, rejected, cut off, and disconnected from a range of behaviors, activities, and accomplishments enjoyed prior to the trauma or challenging event. It is important to note that survivors are not the only ones who suffer as a result of trauma. These events touch entire families, friends, colleagues, and communities who also suffer the pain and grieve as a consequence of such events.

September 11, 2001, NYC

*"Just five feet away from me, I hear a voice, 'Come
this way.'" On the ground, under some debris, I find
a fireman. I said, "Are you OK?' He says, "I'm OK,
don't worry about me. Just go down the stairs."*
—Frank Razzano; Marriott World Trade Center complex
after the Twin Towers collapsed in the September 11, 2001

Tuesday, September 11, 2001. Edwin Morales was getting ready for work. His wife had already left for her job in New Jersey at 6:00 a.m. Edwin was busy getting ready to go to work in Queens at 10:00 a.m. He wasn't watching the news. Suddenly, his sister called. He was curious. *Why was she calling so early in the day?* He answered, "Hey, sis, how are you doing? Why are you calling?" "Turn on the news! What is going on in New York City?" she shouted. "What are you talking about?" Edwin asked. Then, he saw it all.

"Both towers were hit, and I went outside and saw them burning. I didn't realize exactly what was going on. I saw people running around, families grabbing their kids out of the school that was right across the street from where I was living. Standing on the roof, I could see both the towers burning then saw the first one collapse." He went back to his apartment. He didn't want to see more of the destruction. "I didn't want to see that image. I called my wife." Initially unable to contact her, he finally got through, but she would not be able to come home anytime soon. The city was completely shut down. All the tunnels, bridges, and subways were closed. "At least I know you're safe," he said. Focused on the New Yorkers who were losing their lives at the time, it wasn't until the next day that he was able to think about his cousin, Ruben Correa, a firefighter assigned to Engine 74 from the Upper West Side in NYC. He knew his cousin would be at Ground Zero. Ruben's engine company was sent straight to the Marriott World Trade Center to search for and rescue guests.

Part of a large and extended family, Edwin desperately tried to get through to Ruben's wife, children—anyone. He couldn't. On September 12th, he learned from cousins and an uncle that "they put him down as missing." Ruben was on the missing list, not presumed dead.

By September 15th, four days after the attack and still hearing nothing from Ruben, Edwin, his wife, sister, aunt, nieces, and nephews tried to get to Ground Zero but were only able to get as far as Battery Park. "We finally made it down, just to get word, some word about what was going on. How is the rescue and recovery going? Any word on Ruben?" Edwin saw a group of firefighters. They knew about Ruben and that he had been at the Marriott. Initially they were not sure of his status—now it was "missing and presumed dead." They searched for his body, and four days later, it was confirmed. Ruben D. Correa was killed. At forty-four years old, a thirteen–year veteran of the FDNY, he was the only member of Engine 74 to not make it home on 9/11.

Guests in the Marriott World Trade Center hotel, located between the towers, were understandably terrified. They didn't want to come out when the towers were hit. A skylight was on the top, the twenty-second floor of the hotel. Not only was debris falling from the towers, but people were jumping, landing on the skylight and falling to their death trying to escape from the towers. Ruben and other firefighters made it to the twenty-second floor, found guests, and were given orders to "get them [the guests] and get out." A line of firefighters and hotel guests began moving toward the stairs to the exit. Ruben was at the back of the line, making sure they were moving together and all were accounted for. As they moved toward the exit, the South Tower collapsed, debris landing on the hotel. Only a few feet from the others, Ruben was hit and overtaken by the debris. The group continued down the stairs and made it to a small area between the second floor and the hotel lobby. The "shoe box," as it was called, did not get crushed. If Ruben had just made it a few feet forward on the twenty-second floor, he would have lived. The hotel was torn in half by the collapse of both towers. They never found Ruben, his uniform, or his equipment.

Edwin was told that the firefighters shielded the guests, asking them to pray for Ruben. As they looked up, it was as if someone was holding off the debris so they could all escape. Ruben's partner couldn't explain it. "It felt like Hercules was holding the ceiling up so it wouldn't collapse on them." He couldn't understand why he didn't get crushed, why he and the guests didn't die that day. How were they able to get out? His partner thought that Ruben somehow held up that structure and saved him and the guests they were able to bring with them. It was later noted that after the 1993 World Trade Center bombings, part of the hotel had been retrofitted and reinforced with rebar. However, Edwin shared with me, "That is the scientific explanation, but others believe Ruben's spirit actually prevented that area from collapsing."

Ruben Correa and forty other firefighters lost their lives at the Marriott World Trade Center located between the World Trade Center's North and South Towers. He left a wife and three daughters. One of his daughters had a child not long after he was killed. Edwin said, "It was as if he was reincarnated into that child. They named him Ruben. When we see him, it is like he [Ruben] has never gone." Life for the families goes on, but to them, Ruben will never be gone. "He is my rock, my guardian angel. If I don't have Ruben's picture in my pocket, it is like I am out of uniform."

To honor his cousin and the others who lost their lives that day, every September 11, Army Reserve Sgt. Edwin Morales goes to Ground Zero, the 9/11 Memorial, to pay tribute, remember, and interact with others so he can be healed and heal others; that's how it is. "You meet other people, and they suffer just like me, and you talk to them, and you cry with them and you even laugh with them because you tell them stories of who that person was. And they tell you about their son or daughter."

Edwin himself goes to the memorial on a regular basis. Not all family members can. It is too tough. "But that's OK. Everyone mourns differently." Talking helps, but being totally healed is still not something he recognizes. "You accept it, but the healing part? I will never be healed because of the way he was taken. But talking is a healing process; talking is the best thing to do." He knows you can't hold on to the anger and grief, and he knows, "...people that went through some tragedy, they taught me or they showed me what to do in time of crisis, not to hold it all in."

His spirituality helps as well. "I was raised Catholic, and I believe in God. The Lord is always with me and guides me . . . so you gotta believe it. On days like that, you need God even more."

Finally, Edwin makes it clear that family is key. "I was raised in Brooklyn, and my family was from Puerto Rico. We have a big family in Brooklyn and we have always been close." Ruben was always there, a big presence in the family. All were well connected before this disaster, there for each other during the trauma and afterward. They got stronger through each other. "When we see a family member really struggling, my family will step in." They meet, cry, laugh, and have learned to "take something bad and . . . take the good out of it. Life goes on; you have to."

Ruben and his wife had two teenagers and a baby girl at the time of 9/11. The daughters were close and have stayed that way. The older girls took care of each other, their younger sister, and their mother. Growing up, getting married, and having their own children, all three girls now live in the same city. They continue to look out for and help each other, and now there are seven grandchildren.

Acts of Terror, Acts of Courage

Army Reserve Sgt. Edwin Morales considers his cousin, Ruben D. Correa, from Engine Company 74, FDNY, a hero. "He was always a hero. He was a Marine, always helping people and family. He wanted to be a firefighter to help." Edwin understands that Ruben's remains, as well as his spirit, rest at Ground Zero. "There is no specific burial site or headstone. Our headstone is that waterfall with all those names. In a way, that is the best headstone you could have. You are surrounded with others—people that are connected. When I found out he was missing, then that he was dead, that is what he lived for, to help others, and he died helping. Ruben is probably up there in heaven helping people out."

Vicarious Trauma

Vicarious trauma (VT) is emotional residue that occurs over time, resulting from interactions with and exposure to trauma survivors and their experiences. Accumulation of emotional consequences, even moral distress, can result from working with people who have been through significant pain and adversity. Hearing their stories, sensing their pain, fear, and at times, the terror endured by the survivors can be disturbing for those involved. This is noted in the helping professions, where clinicians and therapists have described it as the "cost of caring," potentially marked by shifts in perspectives and changes in the meaning of the trauma. VT survivors can experience and feel depression, as well as other emotionally concerning signs. Symptoms of posttraumatic stress disorder can result from providing care, gradually changing a clinician's, therapist's, or counselor's internal thought and emotional system. Unlike secondary traumatization syndrome (STS), VT is demonstrated by shifts or changes in perspectives, with intellectual or mental changes regarding life's meaning, beliefs, plans, and adaptations.[45,46]

---

[45]   Figley, Charles R. *Treating Compassion Fatigue. Psychosocial Stress Series, 24.* Brunner-Routledge, 2002.

[46]   Sabin-Farrell, Rachel, and Graham Turpin. "Vicarious traumatization: Implications for the mental health of health workers?" *Clinical Psychology Review, 23(3),* 2003. 449–480.

Secondary Traumatization Syndrome

Secondary Traumatization Syndrome (STS) is slightly different. It involves emotional duress that occurs suddenly and unexpectedly. This is a more generalized distress seen in people who share close relationships with survivors of traumas and significant challenges, like Edwin. Specifically, STS involves a situation in which the person, not the principle victim and not directly hurt by the trauma but in close proximity or hearing a firsthand account of a trauma experience, develops psychological setbacks and symptoms similar to those experienced by the survivor.[47,48,49] Exposure to traumatized individuals and the indirect contact to troubling issues and experiences can also bring forth emotional and psychologically distressing symptoms similar to those experienced by survivors.[50] STS can also include symptoms similar to PTSD: intrusive thoughts, flashbacks, avoidance behaviors, and sleep disturbances.[51,52] Some examples of STS include my own family and those on the pool deck when I was being resuscitated, witnessing a car accident (especially if someone was tragically hurt), September 11,

---

[47] Sabin-Farrell, Rachel, and Graham Turpin. "Vicarious traumatization: Implications for the mental health of health workers?" *Clinical Psychology Review, 23(3)*, 2003. 449–480.

[48] Greene, Talya, Yael Lahav, Israel Bronstein, and Zahava Solomon. "The role of ex-POWs' PTSD symptoms and trajectories in wives' secondary traumatization." *Journal of Family Psychology, 28(5)*, 2014. 666–674.

[49] Galovski, Tara, and Judith A. Lyons. "Psychological sequelae of combat violence: A review of the impact of PTSD on the veteran's family and possible interventions." *Aggression and Violent Behavior, 9(5)*, 2004. 477–501.

[50] Greene, Talya, Yael Lahav, Israel Bronstein, and Zahava Solomon. "The role of ex-POWs' PTSD symptoms and trajectories in wives' secondary traumatization." *Journal of Family Psychology, 28(5)*, 2014. 666–674.

[51] Adams, Richard E, Joseph A. Boscarino, and Charles R. Figley. "Compassion Fatigue and Psychological Distress Among Social Workers." *American Journal of Orthopsychiatry, 76(1)*, 2006. 103–108.

[52] Galovski, Tara, and Judith A. Lyons. "Psychological sequelae of combat violence: A review of the impact of PTSD on the veteran's family and possible interventions." *Aggression and Violent Behavior, 9(5)*, 2004. 477–501.

active duty soldiers, and first responders—anyone in close proximity to such events.

Traumatic experiences individually, vicariously and secondarily bring forth problems, but they can also, over time, bring about resilience, grit, and growth. The following will define, explain, and reveal how vicarious and secondary traumatization survivors can also experience posttraumatic growth (PTG).

> *A society cannot make do with only talking about victory. We always say that we learn more from defeat than from victory. So, if we learn from defeat, we should pay a bit more attention to those who lose.*
> —Ron Shelton, Documentary Film: *Losers*

In all areas of life—physical, mental, emotional, and spiritual—the capacity for growth in the aftermath of challenges and crises is recognized as a potential outcome; however, it is important to appreciate that the event itself is not what brings resilience, grit, and growth. The lessons and behaviors, including adaptation, as well as enhanced coping mechanisms and abilities, are consequences of purposefully and courageously responding to and *engaging* with the struggles and challenges brought forth by the trauma. Beginning with my experience, adding other survivor stories, plus books and films—even poems—I started to understand and appreciate the human capacity for using challenges, struggles, and traumas to learn life's important lessons. Events that bring forth pain and suffering also bring forth personal meaning and promote growth. The trauma itself is not what brings resilience and growth; these are acquired as a result of taking on and dealing effectively with significant challenges. Initially, I didn't see it or appreciate it; however, once acknowledged, it is a game changer. When faced with adversities, including defeats, losses, and trauma, individuals have the ability and can choose to generate new thoughts, ideas, and superior ways of being; they can grow.

Posttraumatic Growth: Focus on the Positive

For thousands of years, mythological, spiritual, and religious ideologies described the possibility of a positive transformation brought forth through challenges, suffering, and pain. Fairy tales and movies like *The Lord of the Rings, The Matrix, Star Wars, Gladiator, Spartacus,* and *Harry Potter,* to name just a few, have promoted this concept. Poems and books—both fiction and nonfiction—have lauded this ability as well. Becoming better and stronger and positively transforming as a result of surviving *and* effectively responding, engaging with, or taking on tough situations does happen. The pain, suffering, and fear are the vehicles and opportunities that drive the changes and bring forth personal, physical, emotional, and spiritual growth for individual survivors as well as their family and friends. Stop for a moment. Think about what you just read. It is very likely that you can recognize this in yourself, a friend, or family member.

The Science behind Posttraumatic Growth (PTG)

Tedeschi and Calhoun, psychologists and professors of psychology at the University of North Carolina at Charlotte, together pioneered the development of research and theory on posttraumatic growth. For over three decades, they have been studying this aspect of trauma, coining the term "posttraumatic growth" (PTG) to describe this ability and pattern of behavior. Initially they used terms like *perceived benefits, positive aspects,* and the *transformation of trauma,* but eventually preferred PTG. They felt it brought forth the essentials of this phenomenon and the capacity and behaviors of survivors to surpass, move beyond the status quo, and experience improvements to their life as a direct result of how they dealt with the trauma. In general, PTG refers to positive psychological changes that people report as a result of the struggle with difficult and highly challenging life circumstances.[53,54]

Engaging the System

Again, it is essential to note that the event, the trauma alone, does not bring forth PTG. It is the *response* to the trauma in which PTG is unearthed or developed. Tedeschi and Calhoun clearly state that growth does not occur due to the trauma; it is the struggle with the new life—one's new reality after trauma—that determines the ability and extent of PTG. They use the metaphor of an earthquake to describe this concept. When an earthquake occurs, there is shaking, causing damage in several areas of the building, and destruction is determined by how well the structure was to begin with, as well as the severity of the seismic waves causing the quake. There may be little damage, or it may be shaken to its foundation. I think about this as a psychological as well as a physical seismic event. The structures that guide and support personal meaning, controllability, predictability, and understanding of the world could suffer severe damage, challenging one's safety and personal identity. After an earthquake, one of the first activities is the cleanup, closely followed by a full assessment of damage, identifying what can remain, what withstood the shaking, and what did not. A strategy is then devised that includes which areas need to be reinforced or retrofitted to improve or strengthen their ability to withstand another quake. Finally, areas of wide-ranging damage are identified, necessitating a complete tear down and rebuilding of the structure to accommodate and/or withstand future shocks.

[53] Calhoun, Lawrence G., and Richard G. Tedeschi. *Posttraumatic Growth in Clinical Practice.* New York: Brunner-Routledge, 2013.

[54] Lindstrom, Cassie M., Arnie Cann, Lawrence G. Calhoun, and Richard G. Tedeschi. "The relationship of core belief challenge, rumination, disclosure, and sociocultural elements to posttraumatic growth." *Psychological Trauma: Theory, Research, Practice, and Policy, 5(1),* 2013. 50–55.

Think about this in the context of personal trauma. Rehabilitation and recovery strategies are much like the example of the earthquake. Initially, focus is placed on immediate care—what needs to be done in the here and now to ensure one's safety and survival. Then, appraisal of what is standing, what physical structures or abilities can be saved and repaired. Finally, determining what is so damaged that a complete restoration is needed for recovery. This time and assessment allows one to directly incorporate the trauma into established and innovative coping mechanisms (retrofitting), growth mindsets and schemas (replacing) that enhance their understanding of themselves and their world, allowing them to become stronger and more resistant to being shattered in the future. These results are recognized and experienced as PTG. It is not the earthquake but the restructuring and rebuilding that brings forth possibilities for positive personal changes and behaviors that helped them survive, but more importantly, move past their previous baseline to grow, not in the face of adversity, but as a direct result.

I will use my situation to exemplify this idea. There are physical, psychological, and emotional traumas. When I first came into the emergency room, they needed to appraise my physical status—the acute phase, establishing life, including sustaining a heart rate and respirations. Assessing the damage, clearing things out, and identifying what could be saved—what was working and what needed immediate repair or support to sustain life. I was given the emergency care needed, placed on a respirator, and admitted to an intensive care unit (ICU). The beginning assessment is determining what one has that is functional. Although many of my systems were functioning independently, some required extra support and assistance. During my ICU stay, there was ongoing care to keep them going. I was continually monitored and assessed, identifying what worked to support my survival - to keep me alive and then move to the next phase of healing. Eventually it was noted that although key systems were damaged due to the trauma, they were once again able to work, but I needed assistance, almost retrofitting in the form of ongoing care, including cardiac rehabilitation to boost my abilities.

My physical body was assessed and what was damaged, over time, healed without the need for replacement, just maintenance in the form of rehabilitation programs and medication; however, there was emotional and psychological damage needing attention as well. Prior to the trauma, how strong was the structure—in this case, me—in terms of resilience and confidence in handling stress? How significant/severe was the traumatic event? What did I have to work with regarding internal and external support (family, friends, community)? I needed to fully understand my situation and critically evaluate my strengths and abilities to heal and move forward. I needed help to clear out the debris and damage to completely assess what was left for me to use, identify what needed to be supported, torn down, or taken away, and detect what was required to fix the existing structure. Recognizing obstacles that could hamper my healing and growth was also necessary. And finally, over time, it was important to recognize what needed to be removed so I could replace broken or damaged emotional, psychological, and spiritual practices with something stronger and better. This rebuilding would not have occurred unless there was a "quake," a challenge or adversity that initiated and necessitated a response in order to move forward, heal, and grow – allowing one to ultimately experience the domains of PTG.

Five Domains of PTG

Tedeschi and Calhoun's extensive research and interviews of survivors developed *Five Domains of PTG* (1996) to clarify, explain, and measure the experience of posttraumatic growth.

1. *Greater appreciation of life.* Survivors developed significant gratitude for life in general. Simple, everyday joys took on

important meaning; they felt lucky to be here and, at times, changed priorities in their daily routine and life.

2. *Warmer, more intimate relationships with others.* They felt very connected to others, especially those who had a role or supported them during their trauma and recovery. They recognized their "real" friends and had greater compassion and connections with others who shared their same fate.

3. *A greater sense of personal strength or a recognition of possessing personal strength.* In general, they had an "I got this" attitude, feeling better able to handle situations and not stress over small problems.

4. *Spiritual development.* They connected with their religious and spiritual life to help them work through struggles. People who are less religious, even atheist, noted that the engagement of grappling with existential or life questions in and of itself can be a growth experience.

5. *New possibilities.* Personal losses—doors being closed— provided views to other possibilities and discovered passions.[55]

The mindset and ongoing research in this area helps shape more productive and strategic approaches to trauma and rehabilitation, including positive aspects brought forth in the aftermath to include PTG.[56,57,58,59] There is no question that trauma and challenging events

55 Tedeschi, Richard G., and Lawrence G. Calhoun. "The Posttraumatic Growth Inventory: Measuring the positive legacy of trauma." *Journal of Traumatic Stress, 9(3),* 1996. 3455–71.

56 Mikal-Flynn, Joyce. "MetaHabilitation: How to survive life after trauma." *Nursing Times,* 2012. Web.

57 Mikal-Flynn, Joyce. "Posttraumatic growth: Breaking through to recovery." *Nursing, 47(2),* 2017. 48–54.

58 Smith, Daniel J. "Rehabilitation counselor willingness to integrate spirituality into client counseling sessions." *The Journal of Rehabilitation, 72(3),* 2006. 411.

59 Tedeschi, Richard G., and Lawrence G. Calhoun. "The Posttraumatic Growth Inventory: Measuring the positive legacy of trauma." *Journal of*

cause negative and troubling issues. What is also clear is that these events reveal remarkable human potentials, including acknowledgement of personal control, resilience, strength, and insight. Directing the focus of trauma aftercare toward personal strengths, building on personal assets and the potential for posttraumatic growth is a more effective solution to survivors' struggles.[60,61] Research in this field has been aided by scientists using and clarifying survivors' perspectives of trauma to include growth after traumatic and life-altering experiences.[62,63] Effectively engaging with such experiences provides an opportunity to understand who you are but, more importantly, who can you be.

Traumatic Stress, 9(3), 1996. 3455–71.

[60] Park, Crystal L., and Amy L. Ai. "Meaning making and growth: new directions for research on survivors of trauma." *Journal of Loss and Trauma, 11,* 2006. 389–407.

[61] Diener, Ed. "Positive psychology: Past, present, and future." *Oxford handbook of positive psychology,* second edition. New York: Oxford University Press, 2009. 7–11.

[62] Diener, Ed. "Positive psychology: Past, present, and future." *Oxford handbook of positive psychology,* second edition. New York: Oxford University Press, 2009. 7–11.

[63] Hein, Serge, Daniel C. Lustig, and Ayse Uruk. "Consumers' recommendation to improve satisfaction with rehabilitation services: A qualitative study." *Rehabilitation Counselling Bulletin, 49,* 2005. 29–39.

Encountering the Beast: Replacing Mystery with Mastery

Lisa Smith-Batchen is an ultra-runner from Idaho with numerous running awards and accomplishments to her name. I appreciate the mindset she adopted as a result of participating in multi-day, hundred-mile races. She refers to her challenges as "the Beast." "I love the Beast" is her metaphor for really tough tests. She actually welcomes encountering tests to her physical, emotional, and mental abilities. She sees them as opportunities to become stronger and better at responding to the Beast in the future. It lets her know she has pushed herself. Her training provided preparation.

"I actually look forward to the Beast showing up because every time he does, I handle him better. I get him more under control" (Christopher McDougall's *Born to Run*, pg. 125). She discusses having time to mess with the Beast, showing who is in charge, who is the boss. You can't hate something and expect to beat it. You have to go after it. Push forward into it using your past training to guide you, with a sincere and focused commitment to taking on adversity and challenges and meeting them head on with personal strengths.

"Meeting the Beast" is the best of PTG. Philosophers, scientists, theologians and people like Lane, Sally, Ashley, Alma and Edwin, who shared their stories in this book, remind us to truly grow from difficult situations; you must go after it. This ability and behavior reflect an evolution, a development of a person's mindset allowing them to resist, go beyond, and become over time, less affected or damaged by highly stressful situations. Use of prior traumas and challenges has refined and mastered coping and adaptation skills, lessening the mystery and fear of troublesome experiences, allowing one to better address threats. Practicing and modeling these behaviors and mindsets from the beginning can also prepare children to become more resilient, stronger, and ready to face future adversity.

The Paradox: PTG Can Coexist with Pain and Grief

The paradox of PTG is to fully recognize that profound gains and profound growth can come in the midst of profound loss. As Drs. Tedeschi and Calhoun and other researchers remind us, through vulnerability comes strength and, over time, wisdom. But this knowledge and growth came with a price.[64,65] While survivors of significant challenges identify the growth brought forth, they still experience pain, grief, and distress. If Lane could turn back the hands of time and walk again, he would; however, that wish doesn't mean he has not experienced PTG. He has come to realize that although he has limitations in mobility, there are things he can and wants to do, and there are adaptations that allow him to still engage in meaningful and fun activities.

As noted with other survivors, this life change also opened up a new career path. He finished his degree and is considering teaching. The event was unwelcomed, but the growth and personal knowledge it brought forth is invaluable. His limitations lead to a willingness to explore and identify new opportunities, and his recovery provided the strength of mind to take them on. Over time, growth happens as the survivor bravely engages with the event and encounters the Beast, feeling the power and mastery brought about by focusing on the gains rather than the losses. *They get it.*

It is important to remember that this concept or practice of taking on life is not unique to survivors of major traumas. It may be more acutely felt and noticeable in the aftermath of these significant events, but remember, this mindset can result from thoughtful engagement with lesser daily difficulties of life. Pay attention to doors closing, disappointments, and failures, and use these situations as motivations to explore and try new things.

---

[64]   Tedeschi, Richard G., Lawrence G. Calhoun. "Posttraumatic growth: conceptual foundations and empirical evidence." *Psychological Inquiry,* 15, 2004. 1–18.

[65]   Westphal, Maren, and George A. Bonanno. "Posttraumatic Growth and Resilience to Trauma: Different Sides of the Same Coin or Different Coins?" *Applied Psychology: An International Review,* 56(3), 2007. 417–427.

Vicarious and Secondary Trauma Survivors and PTG

It is important to note that family and friends of trauma survivors, as well as clinicians who work to help heal those who have experienced troubling issues, can also experience PTG. Research and personal interviews provided evidence that when faced with challenges, secondary and vicarious trauma survivors also grew, using their experiences, working to generate new and positive thoughts, ideas, and behaviors. Discussions with my own family members, as well as others profiled in this book, revealed that they found benefits during and after the traumatic events they were involved in, at times, even in the midst of their suffering.

Trauma therapists and clinicians, a subset of clinical work, is emotional and extremely difficult; however, research finds they can also be enriched, receiving positive benefits as a result of their work with survivors. Vicarious posttraumatic growth occurs, bringing about changes in people's lives and attitudes in profound ways. Those providing care and services experienced positive changes, that included increased self-perception, better interpersonal relationships, and a more positive outlook and philosophy of life after their interactions with trauma survivors.[66,67,68] Specifically, therapists noted feeling more compassion, having better insight, tolerance, and

---

[66] Bauwens, Jennifer, and Carol Tosone. "Posttraumatic growth following Hurricane Katrina: The influence of clinician's trauma histories and primary and secondary traumatic stress." *Traumatology, 20(3)*, 2014. 209–218.

[67] Tedeschi, Richard G., Crystal L. Park, and Lawrence G. Calhoun. "Posttraumatic growth: Conceptual issues." *Posttraumatic growth: Positive changes in the aftermath of crisis.* New Jersey: Lawrence Erlbaum Associates, 1998. 1–22.

[68] Hein, Serge, Daniel C. Lustig, and Ayse Uruk. "Consumers' recommendation to improve satisfaction with rehabilitation services: A qualitative study." *Rehabilitation Counselling Bulletin, 49*, 2005. 29–39.

a deeper appreciation of the resilience of the human spirit—actually marveling at the strength of the human spirit.[69,70]

> *Nobody is gonna hit as hard as life, but it ain't how hard you can hit. It's how hard you can get hit and keep moving forward. It's how much you can take and keep moving forward. That's how winning is done.*
> —*Rocky*, Rocky Balboa gifts

Conclusion

I would add to Rocky's statement, "That's how growth is done." Using my life experience as motivation and a guide to glean deeper knowledge regarding the aftermath of trauma, I offer you a realistic picture of both challenges *and* important lessons involved in trauma. Positive outcomes, including personal growth, resilience, better relationships, feelings of power, and accomplishments can arise from the most desperate of situations. Traumas are not end points. They are the beginnings to another life. It takes extensive time and disciplined effort as well as being fully engaged in the recovery process from the outset. It is also key to recognize the potential for PTG at the start. Being aware of what one can do, taking control, realizing traction and successes, and reaching out for help and support is fundamental to the eventuality of PTG.

I didn't understand it initially, but as a survivor, clinician and researcher, I came to appreciate knowledge required experience, new ideas, and supportive data that came in parts, in stages, much like the

69 Ramos, Caterina, and Isabel Leal. "Posttraumatic growth in the aftermath of trauma: A literature review about related factors and application context." *Psychology, Community & Health, 2(1)*, 2013. 43–54.
70 Arnold, Debora, Lawrence G. Calhoun, Richard G. Tedeschi, and Arnie Cann. "Vicarious Posttraumatic Growth in Psychotherapy." *The Journal of Humanistic Psychology, 45(2)*, 2016. 239–263.

process of survival and life afterward. It didn't happen overnight; it came with time, effort, and a fierce determination to improve my situation and that of others, adding pieces to the puzzle brought greater clarity and personal understanding to the trauma experience. PTG is one of those pieces. The perceptive and thoughtful work of Drs. Richard Tedeschi and Lawrence Calhoun provided the term and concept of "posttraumatic growth," and the Five Domains of PTG describing the personal transcendence possible in the aftermath of trauma.

My experience spurred an interest in other disciplines and research, like those mentioned in the chapters on stress—resilience, genetics, happiness, and gratitude—giving me more ideas, opening possibilities and potentials in the aftermath of trauma. Awareness and knowledge of these scientists and their research influenced, and continues to influence, my pursuit to more fully understand the survivor's journey, filling me with both inspiration and hope that my work provides useful answers to difficult problems. I wanted to do the heavy lifting, releasing some of the burden faced by survivors, their family, and friends. Part Three will do just that by introducing a strengths-based model of recovery - a specific road map that engages the survivor, identifying their abilities and grit in *moving forward* toward a productive recovery and the experience of PTG.

Chapter Contributors
Richard Tedeschi PhD, professor of psychology at the
University of North Carolina at Charlotte
Ryan Tweltridge, Captain, Sacramento Fire Department

PART THREE

PART THREE

CHAPTER 7

METAHABILITATION: A STRENGTHS-BASED SYSTEM OF RECOVERY

rauma and crisis are inescapable aspects of life. Some are more brutal than others. Modern medicine is powerful, and with sophisticated and constantly evolving technology and pharmacology, there is a more optimistic outlook for survival from many significant diseases, traumas, even catastrophic events. However, as mentioned earlier, my experience, research and that of others, identified current rehabilitation models as limiting, tending to focus on what is wrong and the problems associated with recovery. Let me be clear, there is no question problems occur and are necessary to address, however, there are other aspects of the recovery process that need to be included in aftercare as well. The human spirit must be taken into consideration, the survivor's willingness and capacity to face, overcome and, over time, derive meaning and grow from the experience when provided an opportunity and clear direction. I do not suggest that the medical model be discarded or eliminated, but it has limitations. As a more balanced approach toward trauma research has occurred, allowing a better understanding of survivors' potentialities and possibilities, it is also necessary to take that balanced approach with aftercare. Therefore, to address limitations, reduce burdens associated with trauma, engender hope and support survivors and their families toward a more productive recovery, I created a contemporary rehabilitation system: *metahabilitation* (metahab). This system and clinical pathway uniquely engages the survivor, prioritizing their expressed needs and stated goals, focusing on their resilience, personal strengths and capacity for growth.

Part One of this book introduced you to the importance and necessity of the topic, using my story as background and identifying my motivation to bring about change. Part Two provided scientific evidence supporting a more balanced approach to rehabilitation, focusing on what survivors can do, specifically leveraging internal systems and capacity to stimulate and build resilience, personal strengths and promote productive outcomes including PTG. Now, Part Three will put you to work. Metahabilitation, the word and concept, is described, revealing how it all unfolded. Next, the specifics of this strengths-based recovery system, including characteristics and facilitating conditions supporting a productive outcome in the aftermath of trauma is presented. After reading this content in its entirety, I encourage you to take time and directly apply the system to your own situation and experience. "Stage" yourself, and see what characteristics and facilitating conditions you have that support and guide your recovery process and growth. Recognize where you are and what can help you move forward. This system and process was built for ease of use. Take it on. You may want to engage the support and insights from trusted friends, family or therapist to review the stages and identify the characteristics and facilitating conditions which helped guide you forward. Enjoy the journey, your journey. *You got this!*

A Singular Focus: Challenging and Changing the System

Impossible is just a big word thrown around by small men who find it easier to live in the world they've been given than to explore the power they have to change it. Impossible is not a fact. It's an opinion. Impossible is not a declaration. It's a dare. Impossible is potential. Impossible is temporary. Impossible is nothing.
—Muhammad Ali

I needed to *challenge the system* and change the basic premise and way we think about rehabilitation and recovery—to focus on what we have, what we can do and how survivors must, to the best of their ability, take on what seems impossible by first believing in themselves and then taking control. *We got this*, I kept thinking. *We really do.* Not overnight but over time, with keen determination and support to develop and encourage a growth mindset, hope and grit, survivors move forward and ultimately grow as a direct result of challenges and adversities. I do not minimize the process. Clearly, it is not easy or without pain. But as I became more familiar with this mindset and behavior, I found myself seeing it everywhere—in recreational and professional athletes, soldiers, historical figures, inventors, businesses, artists, scientists, and social justice advocates—individuals like Michael Bentt, Steve Jobs, Elon Musk, Rosa Parks, Thomas Edison, Dr. Martin Luther King, Jr., Malala Yousafzai, Jim Abbott, Jesse Owens, Michael Durant, and Maya Angelou to name just a few. I studied and understood behavioral patterns in their lives and how they approached crises systematically. I turned my attention closer to home, taking time to observe family, friends, neighbors, patients, and students. I recognized that all sorts of people went through bad situations, and with time, acquired skills, they got stronger, and used troubling experiences to move forward and back into life. They saw things differently; they got it. They had setbacks, many times major ones, but they built within themselves a positive and optimistic inner dialogue that brought forth toughness, optimism and well-adjusted personal beliefs in their abilities. They still struggled but became better, more proficient in their response after each setback. Like a prizefighter, they got knocked down, they fell, but they got up more quickly, bouncing back and becoming stronger and more resilient with each punch, each failure. Adversities and let downs were opportunities for growth, to finally get it right. It is vital to note that taking on or adhering to such an attitude or mindset in no way negates the sadness and grief troubling and traumatic life events bring forth. There are tragedies that one does not "get over." I think this is an oversimplification and minimizes the true healing and recovery process. What I am proposing, and what history and research tells us, is that when one chooses to take on life and all the angst and perils that comes with it, they also choose to *use* these events to motivate and fuel their movement forward, to acquire lessons about life and their abilities, realizing the profound meaning brought forth by the crisis, trauma, and adversity.

A Broken Bone Provided Clarity

Have you ever broken a bone? Or needed sutures for a cut or laceration? Let me use these injuries as examples of how our body becomes stronger as a direct result of wounds and trauma. A patient of mine fractured his tibia. He had been evaluated, X-rayed, and casted, then came to see me for his six-week follow-up visit. During his recovery, he had several X-rays to monitor and assess the healing process of his fracture. There were multiple films revealing the acute fracture, one week later, three weeks later, then a current X-ray at six weeks. As I studied the series with my colleague, evaluating if the fracture had healed enough to remove the cast and send the patient to physical therapy, I found myself almost fixated. It was there right in front of me, reflected in the healing process of the bone. In each film, I saw images of myself and other survivors. Even though a bone is strong, it may fracture or break if subjected to excessive weight, sudden impact, or stresses from an unusual direction. Most fractures heal, even after severe damage, provided that the blood supply and the cellular components of the bone survive; however, initially after a fracture occurs, whether partial or complete, extensive inflammation occurs and a hematoma (bleeding and bruising) develops. Things can actually become worse before they improve—and that is *expected;* that is part of the healing process. Next, an internal and external mechanism produces cells that stabilize the bone. These cells are replaced by new bone. Fragmented ends are united. With appropriate therapy, time, and rest, this region will naturally be remodeled and little evidence of the fracture will remain. The recovery may continue, almost unnoticed, for up to a year. If the initial injury is properly attended to, allowed to heal properly, and good choices are made regarding care and activity, the site of the fracture becomes *stronger* than the surrounding bone. Years later, an X-ray of that same area will reveal a thin line where the fracture occurred, but if supported correctly, the repair of the bone is complete. In that one spot, it becomes virtually unbreakable. It is stronger in the aftermath of the trauma.

Lacerations, or cuts to the skin, behave in a similar manner. Things may look very bad, even become worse directly after the laceration. Bleeding, inflammation, and disfigurement can initially occur, but with appropriate treatment choices, healing does occur. The better the treatment, the better the healing; however, many times a small scar is left. Scar tissue is actually stronger than the surrounding tissue; it is tougher. Even germs mutate into stronger strains to survive. Whole ecosystems reflect this capacity. As I continued to contemplate and understand this process, I recognized it virtually everywhere. I noted similar transformations and enhanced healing in all areas of my clinical practice and life. Patients I cared for and other survivors I read about and interviewed experienced healing, not just for the purpose of survival but to ward off future invasions to their homeostasis and overall health—and they became stronger. With more analysis, discussion and research, the full concept of metahabilitation took shape.

Expectations

Strength does not come from physical capacity.
It comes from indomitable will.
—Mahatma Gandhi

Many times, prior to a traumatic life event, we don't recognize, or we underestimate, our potential to deal with adversity. This is why in the beginning, and when making significant changes, survivors struggle and become dependent on others. Although this is normal, an expected part of recovery, if these issues are not appropriately addressed and survivors are not refocused to take control by making choices and identifying personal strengths, this dependency can cause serious disempowerment and long-term difficulties. Furthermore, it is absolutely essential to acknowledge grief, fear, presumed and real limitations, confusion, frustration, and mental and physical pain as anticipated post-trauma issues. These struggles are not out of the ordinary; they are expected and should be planned for in the aftercare. Had these recovery issues been presented as an *expected* part of the process, it would have made a major difference in the amount of time I spent despairing as opposed to digging in my heels, taking control, and moving forward. An awareness, along with strong support concentrating on survivors strengths and abilities, is required to effectively deal with them.

Metahabilitation©: The Word

Things aren't beautiful because of how they sound.
They're beautiful because of what they mean.
—Edith Bratt Tolkien

Researching and developing a clearer understanding of one's remarkable healing capabilities caused me to become dissatisfied, not only with the system but even with the words "recovery" and "rehabilitation." They were insufficient, small, failing to describe or explain capacities and potentials—including strength, choice, and growth—

in the aftermath of injury and trauma. *Merriam-Webster* defines rehabilitation and recovery as:

> "...the action of restoring something that has been damaged to its former condition and recovery as a return to a normal state of health, mind, or strength; the action or process of regaining possession or control of something stolen or lost."

These words are limiting. They are inadequate because they fail to describe what can happen in the aftermath of challenges and trauma. They merely frame the beginning and middle process of healing and should not be accepted as an outcome. I view growth as a conceivable outcome - feeling that survivors are completely capable of achieving PTG.

This failure and lack of understanding to fully identify and describe the potential, capacity, and drive of the human spirit caused me to fashion a new word describing this aptitude and potential. I literally spent hours, days, and months thinking about this. Finally, one afternoon while tossing around the idea with colleagues, someone mentioned the Greek term *meta*, which means "to change a position or condition, to *move beyond*". That was it. The word Metahabilitation was created. It joins two words: *meta*, "to move beyond," and *habilitation*, "to restore something that has been damaged." The word metahabilitation (metahab) provides an appropriate definition and concept of what potentially occurs in the aftermath of challenges, injuries, and trauma: the expressed ability to overcome and be transformed *by* events. The specific meaning "to move beyond restoration, to move past a previous state of being" reveals a paradigm shift in the recovery process and journey. As described earlier, it is noted in the biophysical world and is especially recognized in humans. The capacity to surpass baseline, gain strengths in all areas—physical, spiritual, and emotional—and with time, make productive choices and bolster determination to rise above, move beyond, and metahabilitate.

The Metahabilitation System and Model Emerged

Metahabilitation began with a personal experience and frustration that brought forth critical observations involving first myself then others regarding the ability of challenging, even traumatic, events to bring forth growth. This growth opportunity and outcome is guided by valid and identifiable stages.

The word, its definition and concept, were now clear and it needed to be put into practice so survivors, clinicians, and therapists could use it. In-depth scrutiny of survivor's stories revealed six definite and identifiable stages to this system. Narratives included a young mother of three who had been diagnosed with breast cancer, a gentleman who endured years in Nazi concentration camps during WWII, a young rugby player who became a paraplegic after a car accident, a woman who suffered significant trauma after falling from a thirty foot cliff, a dentist who suffered paralysis after a deep-sea diving incident, and a gentleman with over twenty years of sobriety from a drug and alcohol addiction. I could see the universality of this concept and system. Noted in both the men and women of different ages and different traumas, I heard similar messages and strategies. Through their amazing stories, I heard not only the motivation but, more importantly, the *how*. Their recounting of personal backgrounds, the events they experienced at the time of their diagnosis or trauma, and the aftermath revealed clear tactics and a system. They did not do this in a haphazard fashion. I could see it, almost like a yellow brick road laid out before me—an organized route, a pathway that recognized the obstacles but utilized specific and identifiable strengths to move forward. It was a guide supported by resilience, self-reliance, self-knowledge, and eventually the motivation for mastery and growth. Metahabilitation became more than a clever word or a point of view; it was recognizable as a calculated system and pathway allowing survivors to follow, transitioning from one stage to the next, becoming stronger with each and able to move forward – to grow.

Metahabilitation is designed to be simple, useful and insightful, helping to navigate your survival journey productively. Relying on self-reflection to determine where you are, identifying positive characteristics and personal strengths, strategizing plans for transition to the next stage and ultimately reaching Stage 6. I suggest you use the process frequently as you work through more minor, less toxic struggles and troubles, training for more substantial challenges. The Mikal-Flynn Metahabilitation Model© visually highlights the progression of the six stages. Enjoy your journey...*you got this!*

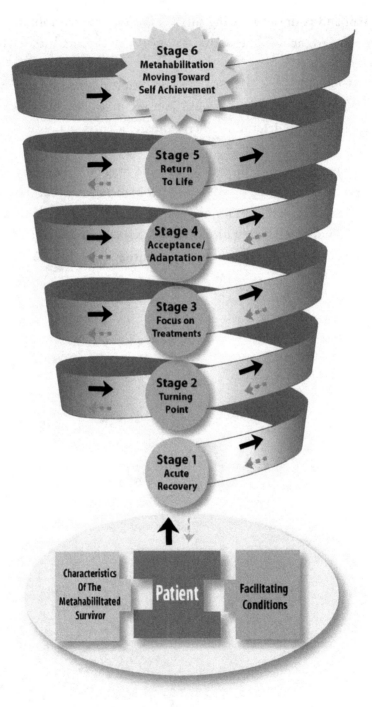

Mikal-Flynn Metahabilitation Model ©

A Pathway Metahabilitation: A Strengths-Based System of Recovery

Survive*Adapt*Amaze

First, early in research, a problem is identified and then a solution is sought.
—Edward O. Wilson, *Letters to a Young Scientist*

Having identified a problem and sought a solution, I would like to share this information with you. My ideas and work regarding this solution came in phases. The concept and phenomenon came first, creating a word to precisely define the activity and ability came next, and finally, a system to achieve metahabilitation was developed.

Speaking to you directly, let me take you through the six stages of metahabilitation, educating you regarding this strengths-based system and guiding your course of action after your trauma, adversity or challenge.

Six Stages of Metahab

Stage One: Survival—Acute Recovery

The Ending Brings Forth Your Beginning.
—Joyce Mikal-Flynn

This stage marks the critical start of your healing journey. It begins as one part of your life ends and the other begins. All attention and focus are concentrated on the now: your immediate survival and getting you through the next minute, hour, or day. Sometimes this involves family or loved ones in the aftermath of an event when the person did not survive. Depending on the event and whether it is physical or psychological, acute intervention of those most involved takes precedence.

Life changed, sometimes drastically, and there needs to be a full-court press to get through this phase. This is not the time to look too far forward. There will be a lot of unknowns and questions. Right now, take a deep breath and focus on the problems at hand. Many things are being done to and for you, perhaps without your awareness, and much of it is not under your control. The clear emphasis is to stay alive and deal with the acute aftermath of the adversity. In my case, resuscitation efforts took more than twenty minutes at poolside, then I was transferred by life-flight to a hospital, put in the ICU on a respirator, and eventually was transferred to another hospital—and I remember none of it. I was fortunate. I had a lot of people looking out for me and making sure what needed to be done was being done. Once home, I do remember feeling exhausted and sleeping most of the day. My body was physically battered, with damage to so many systems, and sleep, an integral part of the healing process, was essential. This applies to emotions as well. Let them rest a bit; don't ask too much from yourself initially. Rest, relax, and take time to recuperate.

Other aspects of this stage include fear, grief, and anger. Much of the anger is due to fear and frustration. This is clearly a time when you need to rely on others who you trust to advocate for you and your care. This is a demanding and very rough time. If possible, I strongly suggest you do not go it alone. Seek and accept help, including emotional assistance. It is smart to let others know you need help. Grief because of an altered life, as well as depression and anger, are all anticipated emotions and parts of the healing process. If you are experiencing any or all of these issues, you are not alone. Initially when discussing some of these problems, I would use the word "normal" and refer to "normalizing" when attempting to describe this process. I no longer do that because I don't want you to consider this to be a normal or ongoing future state. I now identify such issues as recovery and trauma problems and as *expected* components of the recovery, the rehabilitation *process*. These are not end points but a beginning to the entire process. I reassure survivors and their families that I expect them to experience these feelings and go through frightening times. Life has upended you, and these reactions must be judiciously and effectively addressed to continue the healing process. Seek help, but make sure the help you get recognizes that you do not need to be completely "fixed" for you to begin moving forward. More than likely, as you continue your journey, you will recognize your power and strength again; however, these emotions may recur as you move forward, try new things, or are reminded of the trauma. Recognize these recurring emotions as triggers, things to address to keep going, because you need to keep going. Again, these are important and anticipated emotions, and there will be times when you need to step back and deal with emotional and physical issues, but it does not mean you can't or won't move forward. It means you are just being clever about what helps you transition. Continue healing and keep moving. *You got this.*

Stage Two: Turning Points—Saying Yes to Life

Courage is found in unlikely places.
—J.R.R. Tolkien

This next stage is vital; it is key. Saying "yes" to life doesn't mean all is well, it just means you made the critical and courageous choice to move forward. In the midst of fear, sadness, and confusion, you made the fundamental decision that somehow, some way, you *will* move forward. You choose to take life on and do what is necessary to go after a future, your future. In my many years of listening and working with survivors, as well as my own experience, it is not always clear where this courage and determination comes from. But the survivor distinctly remembers almost the exact day and time when they make the vital choice to move forward despite anxiety and fear.

An example I shared earlier, with hard work and the assistance of speech and communications therapists and my great friend and clinical colleague, Dr. Dan Fields, I returned to work on a limited basis. I made the choice to move forward and began doing what was necessary to progress, but it was tough. I had come a long way, but I was not completely myself yet, and I could feel it. One day after work, while driving home on the freeway, I thought to myself, *this is too hard. I don't know if I can do this, if I can really come back.* I saw an embankment and for a split-second thought, *if I just ran into it, it would be all over. I wouldn't have to suffer any more.* Luckily, in that same split second, I thought about my children and my husband. I made, for a second time, the choice, the decision to live and move forward. I remember it like it was yesterday. You need to be brave and decisive, making many other decisions as you progress in the aftermath of your challenge or trauma, but this initial decision, the choice to endure and face the future, is crucial. This key and fundamental choice sets you on a trajectory that informs and motivates you, putting life and what is ahead of you on notice: *you got this.* Now move forward to the business and process of figuring out what you need to get better and stronger, and work hard to get your life going in a positive and productive path.

Stage Three: Treatments—Conventional and Complementary

You can get busy living or you can get busy dying.
—Tim Robbins as Andy Dufresne,
The Shawshank Redemption

Get a team; you will need it. You decided to move forward and now you, your family, and friends are involved in seeking and analyzing treatments—whatever helps bring healing, recovery, and ultimately a resolution. This time is a very busy, active, and engaging stage for you and your supporters. All are researching and advocating for your care, incorporating conventional and complementary interventions. Both are helpful and can be synergistic in terms of effects. Be optimistic but not foolish. Refrain from going with gimmicks that promise a quick fix. Be sensible, trust your gut, and remain open to suggestions from reliable sources. You may already be involved in a host of therapies, but grab hold of the process and be creative. Suspend your pride. Something significant occurred, perhaps bigger than you have ever dealt with before. This is another time when survivors and families do well by reaching out, asking for and accepting help. Seeking help and advice is not a weakness but a strength. You don't want to do this alone. You do not have all the answers, and spending the time and effort to find them, as well as engaging others in that process, is a good thing. You are enthusiastically involved in activities that help you heal, adapt, and continue to move forward, increasing your sense of control and self-confidence. Involving others in the ongoing process of seeking and utilizing therapies will allow you to direct your energy toward the healing process, providing necessary social connections and support.

Push yourself. Push boundaries. Become very strategic and disciplined in your recovery efforts. Set schedules and goals. During this time, you will have definite successes. Celebrate how far you have come and *use* that as motivation to keep going. There will also be times when you fail, but always remember: that doesn't mean you are a failure, only your attempt was. Be optimistic and use these failed attempts as chances to get it right. Take control at every opportunity possible. Document your work, keep track of how far you have come, and set future goals for yourself. Remember that focus, optimism, and control are key. This will not be the last time you spend time on this stage. As you learn more and move forward, you may come back to this stage, but you have now developed a growth mindset and productive strategies, so remember, *you got this.*

Stage Four: Acceptance and Adaptation— A Time to Reflect

It is not the most intellectual of the species that survives; it is not the strongest that survives; but the species that survives is the one that is able best to adapt and adjust to the changing environment in which it finds itself.
—Charles Darwin

Acceptance, adaptation, and reflection are the roots of stage four. Adaptation involves a modification or process involving change in which an organism or person becomes better suited to its environment or situation. You have just come off a significantly busy time. Therapies have been employed, you and others have worked very diligently in keeping you alive and moving forward, and now you need a breather. You have all been through so much. Review what you are adjusting to and make appropriate adaptations for current conditions.

This is a critical time for self-reflection. To gain personal and necessary insights, try to remove yourself from the familiar. Go to a different surrounding or setting, taking time out of regular routines to assess your status and reflect on all that has happened to you. This can be achieved by doing something as simple as going to a park or doing a more complex outing, like an extended vacation. Be as creative as you can with whatever situation you are in, focusing on a setting that helps you gain a positive, healthy perspective.

Other suggested behaviors to help you to ponder and regroup include outdoor activities, journaling, quiet reading, meditation, and utilizing some emotional therapy to promote reflection, personal insight, perspective, and meaning-making regarding the event. Gaining meaning, personal impressions, and resolve in the aftermath of your suffering provides an opportunity to recognize your mental, emotional, even physical strengths and abilities and how this event can be used to inform your future. Viktor Frankl reminds us that,

"In some way, suffering ceases to be suffering at the moment it finds a meaning..." and I would also add, "the moment we find purpose."

Taking control, adapting well, accepting for now, reflecting on the past, but planning and focusing on the future will help you transition to the next stage. Building on your traction, both mentally and physically, brought forth by stage three allows you to look at the adaptations and adjustments necessary to promote and prompt a hopeful future.

During this stage, I adapted and adjusted, taking time to consider the big picture, which helped alter my perspective. I focused, and kept focusing on what I could do, instead of being angry at my limitation or what I couldn't do. I appreciated a return to any measure of physical activity offered to me. During cardiac rehab, I was able to move from walking to jogging and found a range of exercise that felt safe with my heart rate. Over time I started jogging outside of the rehab facility but with a heart rate monitor for my own and my family's comfort. I didn't make a specific "running time" goal. Instead, the time and perspective allowed me to appreciate and find happiness in being active again. Over time, I participated in more activities, but for now, I needed to adapt, adjust, and continue to figure things out. Again, this is not an end point, but it is a necessary stage—a time to assess, begin to find meaning, and gather strength and helpful insights for the next transition.

Life provided you a task—are you addressing it, and how? This is a time to assess and ponder important questions regarding where you have been and how you effectively dealt with the situation. What worked? What didn't? What can you control and change? What adaptations have you made, and what plans do you have for your future? It will not be the last time you consider these questions, but this is a perfect time to start to incorporate it as a practice strategy. Take the time to self-reflect and make sense of what has occurred in your recent past, and think about how that affects a positive and productive future. Next stage, get back into whatever life you can. *You got this.*

Stage Five: Reintegration—Returning to Life

The mountains we climb are not made of only rock
and ice but also dreams and desires. The moun-
tains we climb are mountains of the mind.
—Documentary Film, *Mountain*

This is a transition; for some a more substantial one than for others. You are moving back into life in some manner, although you may not be returning to life at the same level or in the same way you left it. Situations changed you. Challenges changed you. But it is essential to return to some aspect of life. Your energy is restored, and the work you did prepared you for the physical, mental, emotional, and psychological tasks ahead. Taking time to grieve, choosing to move forward, engaging in therapies and treatments, adapting, adjusting, reflecting, and processing what this event has meant allows you to reintegrate and move back into life. You have done the preparation necessary to help reconnect with personal and professional interests. Finding some purposeful work or activity or re-engaging in what you did in the past is essential. To the best of your ability, get back to school, jobs, family, and community. You may realize that even if you go back to life as it was, you tend to see things differently now, with a different perception and approach to your work. This event may have actually pointed you in a completely different trajectory professionally. I have interviewed survivors who moved into careers and work they had always wanted to do but were afraid to leave their job for the certainty they had. Once a door closed due to the traumatic event, they found that other, more interesting and desirable doors opened. These events can be the incentive that allows you to daringly take on unexpected opportunities, activities, and jobs. Consider what you can do, what you want to do, and how to get there.

The traumatic and troubling event provides you with a new outlook, using a different filter or lens to view life. Like me, you understand that life has a timestamp. I completely get life's unpredictability and refuse to waste the time I have on silly and unnecessary drama. I only deal with what I can control, balancing my emotions and focusing on what makes me better able to be helpful to others. The experience you had and the work you accomplished allows you a view from the balcony—a wider, more comprehensive outlook. Although there are differences in the way I engage with life, I now choose to look for ways to fully participate and do the best I can with what I have. Try that yourself. Take what you have learned and boldly move to a productive life. As mentioned, this situation may have opened up an opportunity you always wanted but were afraid to tackle. Over time, that happened in my situation. I question whether I would have gone further in my education or confronted the rehabilitation system had I not dealt with a life-challenging experience. Gaining traction while continuing to work toward improving your situation is key. Although survivors at this stage are still fearful and uncertain about the future, they simply rise above it. Just start somewhere. What plans do you have for re-integrating? Time and life will reveal more as you move forward. Go for it, dive back into life and see what you have to offer. *You got this.*

Stage Six: Metahabilitation— Taking on the Future

> *Personal challenges and struggles have the potential to be an agent of growth, allowing you to face your fears but also recognize the opportunity to turn a tragedy into a triumph.*
> —Joyce Mikal-Flynn

Look at what you created. You have picked up the pieces and put your life back to a place that makes perfect sense for you now. I completely understand that you never chose this crisis or trauma, but you have courageously taken on the challenges and tasks necessary to move forward. Times and situations cannot be changed, only your attitude and approach to it can be altered. Circumstances may not allow you to go back to the life you knew, but this stage signifies your efforts to live your best life, focusing on being happy, productive, and useful. Limitations are not the concern; now it is more about what you can do and how you can be of service.

This stage is unending. It is a way of being, a personal philosophy and structure that guides your life. You have gone through the previous five stages, allowing you to engage in a strengths-based system of recovery that supports a tough mindset and leads to self-confidence and growth in the aftermath of challenging and traumatic life events. Now, *you really got this*. Once you recognize your strengths and create a perception and perspective focused on what you can endure and do and how these situations made you better and stronger, one does not stop there. You do not see limitations or obstacles the way you did in the past. It does not mean you will never feel dejected, pessimistic, or depressed; you just won't stay there because the negativity only serves to keep you down. You have endured, learned, and grown, providing you a more hopeful, optimistic outlook on life. You are more insightful and adept at problem-solving and helping to reach personal accomplishments you didn't see coming when you began this journey. With the assistance of family, friends, clinicians, and therapists, you figured out how to incorporate this thinking, this process and growth mindset, to make successes out of everyday life. Engaging meaningfully in the process, you learned how to live with the unknown; and instead of fighting against it, you leaned in and found how to leverage it to your advantage. Stage 6 on the Mikal-Flynn Metahabilitation Model© reflects limitless activity and open possibilities. There is no stopping you now.

After accomplishing this final stage, you rarely return to the despair noted at the beginning, but you might need to shift back to an earlier stage as you face new challenges. Rest assured, adopting these steps helps you to systematically move through tough life events; however, getting through one event doesn't mean you are exempt from others. Now you have built a specific course of action to take with the next one. Your past successes are foundational, providing guidance and promoting self-confidence as you move on in life and find your purpose. When troubles occur, whether large or small, go back to the basics. Return to the fundamentals. Work through them using the stages to help you successfully move forward with the grace and courage you gained as a survivor.

Finally, ongoing hope, purpose, and service are the hallmarks of this final stage. You understand the pain and the grit needed to move forward—a necessary part of the process and the journey. You evolved, and that personal evolution brought forth resilience, appreciation of life, and a unique perspective and purpose—your purpose for moving on, which is foundational to ongoing growth. As with all heroes' journeys, you need to share your story and positively influence others. *You got this;* now model the way.

Characteristics and Facilitating Conditions of the Metahabilitated Survivor

We are what we repeatedly do. Excellence,
then, is not an act but a habit.
—Aristotle

My research and that of others provided patterns of behavior, specific characteristics, and facilitating conditions found in survivors who successfully navigated through a crisis and trauma. I have listed them for you. Read through them. They are meant to influence and reinforce your healing process. Some may be more helpful than others. Spend time thinking about what can support you and your family in this process. You may recognize underutilized skills and abilities on this list or some you used in the past; dust them off and use them again. Your journey will likely bring you into contact with others who effectively and productively navigated the rough terrain. Engage them in the process and accept their suggestions and guidance. They may show you how to better use your skills, or demonstrate new ones that could make your journey easier.

Characteristics of the Metahabilitated Survivor

Here are observations and information generated from survivors and their stories, regarding the personality traits and mindsets of metahabilitated survivors. When viewing this list, remember that those who achieved extraordinary outcomes are as ordinary as you or I. This information is provided as support to help you deal with trauma in a more straightforward and constructive manner. Take time, review the list, and choose characteristics that you feel apply. There are no right or wrong answers or best numbers. It is your perception of your personal strengths. Don't limit yourself. If you feel you have the characteristic/strength, check it off. Use the list to keep focused and strong as you handle challenges and adversities. Also, feel free to come back to the list and review it more than once. In my work with survivors and their loved ones, people did just that as time went on. Moving their mind in a more positive and productive manner helped them recognize they had more "in them" than they first imagined, giving them further motivation and confidence.

There is some overlap between facilitating conditions and characteristics of the metahabilitated survivor; the latter includes the following:

1. Grateful
2. Hopeful
3. Resilient
4. Optimistic
5. Personal insight (wisdom gained over time regarding themselves and their condition)
6. Ability to focus on possibilities (current and future; continually searched for and were motivated by new opportunities)

7. Follows through on promises to others (vowed they would improve and used these promises as motivation)
8. Defines themselves by their lives post-event rather than by the experience or event itself (the outcome identified them)
9. Adaptation
10. Acceptance
11. Self-awareness (recognized and embraced personal strengths, choices and control)
12. Reflective (took time to contemplate past lives and built new ones)
13. Took control (made productive personal choices regarding care, goals, and life)
14. Surrounded themselves with positive, optimistic people
15. Perceptive regarding positive mindset (refused to live with anger and despair
16. Stopped asking, "Why me?" And instead asked, "Why not me?"
17. Humble (sought and accepted help from others, let go of pride, recognized this was more than they could handle by themselves)
18. Grieved losses but moved on (professional help may be a necessary support for this)
19. Aware (assessed what happened, reviewed where they were, where they are now, and where they want to go)
20. Contributed (found purpose and ways to give back)

Facilitating Conditions supporting the Metahabilitated Survivor

As with stages and characteristics, it is helpful for survivors to gather support from all family members, including spouses, parents, siblings, and grandparents. If this assistance is not available, an alternative is to find and draw needed strength from support groups. These groups, or "families," can help in providing up-to-date information, advocate for care and personal support, and assist you in working through troubling events, especially in the early stages of healing.

The following conditions are powerful supplements to the characteristics that foster and guide the metahabilitation process. Take time to review the list and check off the ones you feel you have. Don't judge yourself. Again, it doesn't matter what you don't have; the focus is on what you *do* have and what you *can* do. As with characteristics, come back later in your healing process and reread them. You may have more coping mechanisms than you initially thought.

1. Family support, both initial and ongoing
2. Positive relationships with family and friends (established prior to the event; came to forefront during times of greatest crisis)
3. Advocacy from family and support groups
4. Willing (or learned) to accept help from others
5. Researched conditions to receive the best and most up-to-date care
6. Went with their gut instinct (made very personal decisions about their care and recovery)
7. Set goals, both short- and long-term, that allowed them to redesign their lives as they chose
8. Stayed away from negative people and thoughts
9. Surrounded themselves with positive people and thoughts
10. Looked at what they could still do. Focused on what they had rather than what they didn't have (A new life unfolds as one comes to terms with what the old life was. This is revisited periodically as survivors come to grips with what they want and do not want in this life. They choose.)
11. Exercised significant control over medical and therapeutic decisions (participated and collaborated in care and choices regarding it)

12. Pushed the envelope (willing, despite fear and apprehension, to try new things in an effort to improve)
13. Pushed personal and preconceived limits
14. Accepted the condition, for now
15. Adapted to the situation and life
16. Spirituality (a sense of a superior power from which to draw strength)
17. Took time to figure things out
18. Grieved losses
19. Got back into life by taking one important step, then another
20. Contacted others with the same problem to learn and give and receive encouragement
21. Found ways to give back; purposeful life (deep desire to make a difference)
22. Recognition of inner strength
23. Hope for the future
24. Recognized the gifts brought forth

Conclusion

A famous Greek maxim is *"Know thyself"* or *"Know your measure."* You have come to the greatest part of your journey, an ongoing focus on life, possibilities, and a future. You look back only to engage and bring forth personal strengths. Dave McGillivray, a highly respected and recognized marathoner, ultra-marathoner, and race director of the Boston Marathon since 2001, jokes that he is so focused on always looking forward that he wishes he could take the rearview mirrors off his car. These experiences, these rites of passage, brought remarkable self-knowledge as you moved and worked through challenging, troubling, and painful journeys. You only look back as a reminder of the strengths and accomplishments that supported, and continue to support, your progression forward.

Now you understand that we create most of our limitations. They are in our mind. We all generate drama, doubts, and fears because our mind can do that. But our mind can also generate a fierce attitude to drive us forward in the midst of challenging, even horrific, events. We are surviving machines. As discussed, we have amazing systems that help us endure and eventually become stronger as a result of physical, emotional, and spiritual assaults. We are created to survive, adapt, grow, and evolve in the aftermath of challenges and traumas, but many times that ability is overlooked or goes unnoticed in day-to-day life. Significant life events bring that out, allowing you to see in yourself and others the best of the human spirit and capability. You will continue to have times when you hit the wall and fall, but once you tune into the new surroundings and take hold of a perspective focused on capacity and ability, you will survive, you will adapt, and your will ultimately amaze. Now you know your measure. *You got this.*

CHAPTER 8

THE ANATOMY OF A SURVIVOR: THE METAHABILITATED SURVIVOR

No dark fate determines the future. We do.
—Dalai Lama and Desmond Tutu in *The Book of Joy*

Why do individuals metahabilitate? What is the exact makeup of a metahabilitated survivor? The following chapter provides information about *why* survivors move forward in a very constructive and positive manner and *how* they are built. Regarding why, simply stated, they say "yes" to a possibility. This is critical. Holding onto a sliver of hope, even in a fragile state, supported by family, friends, and healthcare professionals, they ultimately and over time saw a future, a purpose, and a meaning to their life. Hope led to different thinking. They developed an attitude, a conviction about their future. There is a distinction between potential and actuality. We all have potential, but it is recognizing and embracing personal freedom and control that makes metahabilitation more than just a fancy word. It is a conviction and attitude. Viktor Frankl stated it perfectly, "Everything can be taken from a man but one thing—the last of the human freedoms: to choose one's attitude in any given set of circumstances, to choose one's own way."

After the initial survivor interviews that supported the system and stages of metahabilitation, I spent another fifteen years interviewing and observing hundreds of survivors and their families, reviewed substantial amounts of professional and nonprofessional literature, studied the basics of neuroscience, genetics, and philosophy and watched countless documentaries and films. Aspects regarding how survivors productively and successfully moved forward became clear to me: lives changed, sometimes drastically, but the key to success involves making productive and brave choices, and finally, they developed, overtime, a keen understanding of what the event meant. Throughout the course of recovery, choices were continuously made, however, the first one—the turning point—is vital because it clearly determined their mindset and attitude going forward.

Sometimes the conviction was dependent upon the survivor's own vision and strength. Other times, certainly in the acute stage, it came from others. With each success came more confidence and more control, supporting their drive and desire to push forward. This led to eventual mastery of the situation brought forth by personal contemplation, recognizing where they had come from, what they now had, and an eventual sense of appreciation for insights the event provided. They got it. The pain, fear, and internal distress sustained by the traumatic experience allowed for an opening up of the mind and soul to the truth of what was really necessary and precious in life.

They let go of reckless pride. It quickly became clear that it was foolish to try and go this alone. They needed help, so they asked for and accepted it from a variety of trusted sources and professionals. Insightful and reliable decisions were made that facilitated moving forward in constructive and meaningful ways, prompted by a sense of necessity, urgency, and, at times, fear. They stumbled and suffered disappointments but never gave up; instead, they *used* them as motivation in their recovery.

Metahabilitated survivors live with continual hope and gratitude, hope that they will continue to improve, that they will walk again, run, improve their motor skills, be free of cancer, move past their addictions and dependency, and that they will continue to learn from life's lessons. They feel their lives, even with imposed disabilities or problems, are worth living. They are eventually grateful, profoundly grateful. They are here; they are alive. They chose to enjoy the life they have, perhaps not exactly the way they did in the past, but nonetheless, they are still able to be a meaningful part of others' lives and the world in general. They are better, not bitter.

They developed a pattern of making sound and productive personal choices and continually surrounded themselves with positive thinking, messages, and people. They did not tolerate negativity; they couldn't. They refused to live with anger and despair; it took too much time and energy. They moved on and stopped asking, "Why me?" Instead, they asked, "Why not me?" They chose to define themselves not by the crisis or trauma but, instead, by how they lived their lives afterward. They focused on the rise, not the fall.

They grieved, no question; however, with time, their focus turned to what they had left, what they learned, and how they became stronger. They had lessons to learn and questions to answer, such as: *What am I to make of this? How do I go about living?* Answers to these questions were not always easy or forthcoming. Eventually they recognized the necessity of reaching out and asking for and accepting help in dealing with losses and the intense suffering and anxiety brought about by traumatic life changing events. They sought the insight and support of trusted family and friends, therapists, spiritual guides, and various healthcare professionals, which allowed them to accept, adapt, and see things with more clarity, hope, and gratitude. They let people in instead of always thinking they had to go it alone.

139

They took time to figure things out, sometimes removing themselves from the day-to-day aspects of life to get clarity and free up energy to heal. *What is this all about? Where am I to go now? What am I to do? Who am I now?* If possible, at times, they physically removed themselves from their environments *and* from people who knew them before everything changed. They were different now in many ways and needed to figure it all out without people judging or feeling sorry for them. They needed to get away from small talk and constant questions about what happened. They had much to consider and figure out, and they had plans to make. One day their lives were moving in one direction, and the next, they changed completely. Time and professional help was required to grieve losses and regroup. They made decisions about how to effectively recreate themselves and enter life again.

The Hero's Journey

I consider those who have courageously and thoughtfully moved forward after significantly troubling, tough, and traumatic events to be heroes. At times, their journey is an isolated one and survivors recognized the need to "go it alone" for periods of time. Taking time away, finding special places to rest, recuperate, and spending time in contemplation and reflection are not available to all who face life-changing events; however, this is an important aspect of recovery and growth. When considering a healing place, they didn't center on what was not available, what they couldn't do, or what is not possible. Instead, they looked at what could be done. Focusing on the negative is the reverse of Metahabilitation. Attention must be placed on what is helpful and essential in a complete recovery and how to accomplish this creatively. The necessity of finding some time away and alone to contemplate and self-reflect is important. They were creative and found a place for the purposes of quiet, insightful reflection.

They accepted what was for the time being and moved on. Limitations were noted, but they didn't stand in the way of moving forward and getting back into life. Survivors adapted. They realized they could function with limitations and still do well. At times, those limitations were frustrating, so they studied alternatives and recognized how to overcome obstacles.

They needed and wanted to move on. They did things despite fear and self-doubt, and their success motivated them and led to further successes. As discussed with the growth mindset, these survivors recognized that the effort and the willingness to move forward was as essential as the outcome itself.

Promises were made to themselves and others, giving them tremendous strength and motivation even when facing enormous odds. Surrendering to the situation was, at times, a consideration, but eventually, strength of will and belief in having a future won out. They found a specific focus and reason to come back.

They laughed, helped by families and friends to see the lighter side. They were eventually able to laugh at themselves, and sometimes even at aspects of the situations in which they found themselves. This was essential and allowed them to control and stabilize aspects of their lives.

Survivors rarely give themselves recognition. They are modest and self-effacing, crediting all who surround them with the fact that they did so well. There is actual joy in how they talk about their lives now. Even with their obvious limitations, they have found ways to be happy. Human connectedness—friendships and family relationships—is seen as essential. They lost so much—professions, money, opportunities, bodily functions, and abilities. Their connections and relationships with others were necessary. During their journeys, they recognized the tremendous love and support provided by others until they could do it for themselves. It was clear what real love is all about: feeling an intense and deep connection with family, friends, physicians, and other health professionals who supported and helped them.

The best and most important part of their journey involved self-knowledge. They recognized that sometimes *they* created their limits. We are built to survive, adapt, and grow, but coming back from trauma and major challenges doesn't mean life as it was. It means that you are here, the life you now have is altered, and at times, requiring substantial adaptations, acceptance, and an optimistic mindset for you to move on.

Finally, they *gave back* and continued to do so. As former astronaut Pamela Melroy shares, "In your life's journey, there will be excitement and fulfillment, boredom and routine, and even the occasional train wreck.... But when you have picked a dream that is bigger than you personally, that truly reflects the ideas that you cherish, and that can positively affect others, then you always have another reason for carrying on."

They made their focus about service, many times reaching out to others who had endured similar situations to be of help and guidance. This provided meaning in their lives, gave them a mission and purpose, and took away the pity they may have had for themselves. They recognized how people stepped up, that they were given so much and wanted and needed to return the favor. It made their recoveries more complete. Use what you learned, what you discovered about yourself, as a powerful motivation to feed your dreams, move forward, find meaning in your suffering, and give back. *You got this.*

Cubism and Metahabilitation

Once I saw the capacity of survivors to grow in the face of adversity, I began observing it everywhere, even when visiting a museum exhibiting cubism. Developed by Pablo Picasso and Georges Braque in the early twentieth century, this artistic style and movement abandoned the single viewpoint perspective and, instead, revealed all viewpoints of a person or object at once. This artwork uses cubes and other geometric shapes to show all possible viewpoints or perspectives of the person or object in one frame. A known object is dismantled by the artist and put back together on the canvas. The pieces are there, but the placement of the shapes makes it unique. Although somewhat recognizable, the fragmented shapes and viewpoints make it much more interesting.

As I sat in front of Picasso's masterpiece, *Bowl of Fruit, Violin and Bottle*, I thought about trauma survivors. Lives are crushed, broken down and apart, forcing one to examine every angle, color, and texture and reassemble them into forms we know but struggle to recognize. As with Picasso's painting, the deconstruction is what allows, over time, reconstruction in any way we choose. Things may look different, but the essential pieces are there. Putting lives back together in a way that makes sense is tough, but once one recognizes their ability and chooses to "pick up the dismantled pieces," placing them where they want and allowing for fuller vision and creative license to personalize their picture, they have metahabilitated. They grew; *they got it.*

How Survivors and Their Families Effectively Adapt and Move Forward

I approach all situations believing in the human capacity to achieve this outcome; however, this may not always be the case. It is a bit of an enigma to try and ascertain specifically why some move forward and why others have difficulty and get stuck. It may be due to the enormity of the devastation encountered, a lack of support or guidance, pre-existing situations causing them to struggle more than others or for longer periods of time, overwhelming feelings of hopelessness and despair, or maybe they lack a mindset formed from an early age that recognizes struggles as opportunities and the building blocks that engender personal strength and resilience. However, there is always hope in moving forward and asking for and accepting help as well as using supportive and thoughtful activities is critical and foundational to that ongoing hope.

Check what systems *are working* and how you can better engage them. Ask what the survivor and loved ones see as insurmountable obstacles. Then, take stock. What is available to support and help them? Gather information on past successes, available support, and perceived strengths and personal control.

I completely recognize there are troubling and special situations and times in the healing process that one must seek and ask for help to keep moving forward. I got that help and consider my reaching out a strength not a weakness. I can't emphasize this enough. Traumas overwhelm systems. You are not weak; you are experiencing expected issues associated with the event, and I recommend getting help, special help. It is unwise, almost foolish, even dangerous, to go it alone. Loved ones and friends can be of assistance by reaching out for professional help. Despair leads to depression and isolation. When working with healthcare professionals, veterans, first responders, survivor and family groups, this is one of the first issues I address: *isolation.* I also mention this in the chapter on wellness and mindfulness. I consider it a major red flag. If a family member, client, patient, colleague, or friend is disengaging from life, then action must be taken. If they no longer attend family events and functions, church services, support and social meetings, or work events—basically, if you observe that they have disconnected from normal routines for a period of time—that is a problem and needs to be addressed and dealt with. You may not be the one to do so, but bring someone's attention to the situation. These people are suffering. Leaving them alone to their own thoughts and ideas is not safe. Similarly, if you notice people have been challenged and are not asking for or accepting help, or if they fail to identify joy or purpose in life, support them and help them out. I am not a psychologist or therapist, but with numerous years of experience as a family nurse practitioner and from interactions I have had with mental health professionals discussing these subjects, I know that these issues need focus and special attention.

Anyone Can Metahabilitate

Can anyone metahabilitate? This is one of my most frequently asked questions. My answer is always an emphatic "Yes!" At this point, I am not aware of any specific condition or situation that completely negates the ability of one to experience an enhanced recovery. I trust, and research reveals, that the capacity lies within each of us. As noted, some individuals struggle more due to the significance of their crisis, the overwhelming nature of the event, personal background, or lack of support they have; and again, these specific issues necessitate and require extra help in the form of counseling and other therapeutic care to support the healing and recovery process.

Understanding the conditions and mindsets that enable positive outcomes sheds light on how one accomplishes a productive recovery. The Characteristics and Facilitating Conditions listed in Chapter 7 are intended to assist and support survivors, therapists, and healthcare providers by encouraging and aiding in personal insight and growth in the aftermath of trauma.

Why Do Some People Metahabilitate and Experience PTG While Others Do Not?

I have struggled with this question because I do not see this as a deficiency, and I do not judge individuals' lives after trauma. There are so many unknowns, so many uncertainties. I worry about it more as a lost opportunity to fully understand and appreciate who you are and who you can be. Noted in my and others' research of mental and emotional patterns, behaviors and support systems play an essential role in what motivates and assists one in moving forward. The timing or circumstance may not be right, the support lacking, the suffering too overwhelming, requiring extra, very specialized professional assistance to help heal and begin to move one back into life. In the past I considered my reaching out for help as a weakness. I finally recognized that I would not get through the trauma on my own. I asked for, actually at times, begged, for help. I met my match with this situation, and instead of suffering in silence and going to and remaining in depressing places, I became less stubborn, humbler, and recognized that I needed help to move forward.

Again, it is helpful and important to remember, I did not do this alone. I shared the burden and allowed people in. Humility is a strength. I was honest and told the truth about how scared and angry I was. I didn't overload them, but my family and friends needed to feel that they could help me heal and get me outside help. Ultimately, progress was my responsibility, and I did my part. I worked hard. I listened to suggestions from people who supported me and gave me a clearer viewpoint and clever ideas for how to move forward. As I mentioned, I saw a therapist more than once. I picked a good one who didn't hold me back by focusing on the losses but encouraged and helped me gain a perspective on what this event meant and how to move forward. I grieved the life I lost, the future I thought was now mine, and the intense fear I faced, which helped me gain some understanding regarding what I could do about it. I trusted my gut but also got better at listening to trusted people who loved and cared about me. They suggested, sometimes they almost demanded, that I get help. I recognized reaching out, identifying, and dealing appropriately with obstacles impeding my progress and growth as a sign of strength. Consider reaching out and letting others help you as well.

CHAPTER 9

A ROAD MAP: APPLYING THE METAHABILITATION SYSTEM

The big question is whether you are going to be
able to say a hearty yes to your adventure.
—Joseph Campbell

love road trips. I have taken many, including a couple across the United States. Prior to going on these journeys, I spent time deciding exactly where to start, where I wanted to finish, and the best direction between those two points. I recruited the help of some who had completed trips like these in the past, as well as others who had experience and expertise in this type of travel. Their input helped with choosing the starting point, deciding routes to take, how long I planned to be gone, specific and important sites and people I wanted to visit, and how to build in stretches when I could be alone. There was also time left open for some surprises along the way.

This serves as a perfect metaphor for using the Metahab Model and system. Initially, you need to thoroughly examine and review the six stages and identify your starting point. Then, make a complete assessment of what strengths you have to support you on this journey by reviewing the characteristics and facilitating conditions and checking off all you have. Have others read the information along with you, then go at it as if you are planning a trip and mapping out the course or route you plan on taking. You must have a clear picture of the beginning point and an idea of where you want to end up to know the distance you plan to travel in between, identifying specific routes. As with any road trip, there might be some unexpected detours, a road closure, a storm that sets you back, or a better route to take, but in general, you will have a basic plan that gives you guidance—that is *metahab*. Don't forget, as with any journey, part of the preparation includes making sure you prepared and packed for what is needed. Do you have the important and necessary supplies? Spend time reviewing all your resources/strengths and recognizing what you have to take with you to support you and make your journey better and easier. If you don't have them all, don't worry; you might find them along the way.

Here are three simple steps to take as you plan for and implement your journey. Following this strategy places you in control and focuses on what you want to and can do while considering your abilities and desired personal goals. Basically, make a clear assessment of where you are, where you want to go, how you plan to get there, and what supplies—in terms of personal strengths and coping skills—you have to support your journey.

Step One: Completely review the metahabilitation concept and model, including each of the six stages.

Step Two: Identify your current stage of metahabilitation. Where is your journey beginning? There is no judgment, no right or wrong answer. Simply stage yourself. You can ask others you trust if they agree with your assessment. It is necessary to give your trip a clear starting point to help map out your next steps and provide proper guidance as you transition from one stage to the next, moving toward your final destination.

Step Three: Take stock of your supplies and recognize what you need on this journey. Review the characteristics and facilitating conditions and identify what you have to support your trip. Monitor your internal dialogue; what you say and think about yourself is key. Use the characteristics and facilitating conditions to come from a position of strength. Again, don't make negative judgments or focus on what you don't have; put the emphasis clearly on your assets and abilities. Acknowledging those present allows you to see how personal habits and abilities can help your road trip toward healing and posttraumatic growth.

Have family, friends, therapists, and counselors go through these steps with you. They may recognize things in you that you do not. Include in your analysis a past medical and personal history, especially as it relates to prior challenges and traumas that you overcame in a positive manner. Awareness of past successes and behaviors that led to constructive outcomes is extremely beneficial, as it supports a growth mindset and personal control toward a productive outcome.

You have the power to change your perception of this life experience. To do this, you might need to pull off the road and review the map for clarity. Other times you will need to actually stop and ask for directions, especially on those back roads—the ones less traveled. Again, use trusted friends, family members, and healthcare professionals to provide insights and appropriate guidance on best directions as you are moving forward and transitioning from place to place or stage to stage. This journey is not one to be taken in isolation by only you and a clinician. Families must be involved, as they are a part of the crisis and have a stake in the recovery process. Let them know your specific motivation and goals for taking this trip at this time with this route. Enlist their support, and check in with them along the way. They need to help and keep you safe as you take on your recovery journey.

Ideas for Therapists and Counselors

Metahabilitation is not meant to be a stand-alone therapy or intervention. It is a system, positioned as an additive or adjunct to existing therapies and treatments, to deal with the aftermath of trauma, squarely focusing on personal strengths, control, and choice for survivors, families, friends, and communities as they move forward in a productive manner. I ask clients questions about their past history of trauma, focusing on their successes, perceived personal resilience, and growth. I have them identify and analyze specific features they feel have supported their perseverance, adaptation, and the eventual productive, meaningful outcome. The stage of metahabilitation is determined by the individual client, sometimes using the support of a therapist or clinician and, at times, family insight. Information is acquired as to the presence of each characteristic and facilitating condition.

What follows are the basics of how to incorporate metahab. A more comprehensive description of the system is provided with specific programs and workshops (workbooks and other support can be found at drjmf.com). The purpose of this brief section is to introduce you to the concept allowing for potential integration of the metahab process into your existing practice. Here are three simple steps:

1. Begin helping your client with the critical decision to move forward (the beginning of a growth mindset).
2. Review all stages, characteristics, and facilitating conditions (FCs) and help in staging your client and supporting their identified strengths.

3. Follow the metahab system; use the identified strengths and supports (characteristics and FCs), set goals, and monitor their progression as they use the system, transitioning from stage to stage.

As stages are acknowledged, it is necessary to clarify with clients the specifics of each and discuss how they see themselves progressing through and accomplishing each transition. It is a very interactive process, with attention to defined personal strengths, abilities, and goals supported by self-reflection, self-assessment, and an internal dialogue that focuses on a hopeful and productive outcome decided by the survivor.

My research has not identified an actuarial or specific timeline associated with any of the six stages (see Chapter 7). Individuals usually progress successfully through the stages over the course of several months but note stage six is an ongoing one—an adopted mindset and strategy of addressing future challenges and traumas. Again, progression involves the unique aspects and insights of individuals affected, what they're up against, and their acute and ongoing support. When a lack of progress is noted, it is essential to review the stage, characteristics, and facilitating conditions to help clarify potential forward movement. As noted in the Mikal-Flynn Metahabilitation Model©, 1 many times when new issues occur, survivors attempt new activities or fatigue sets in, causing setbacks; they may slide back (noted with broken arrows)to a former stage before regrouping prior to moving forward once again.

The Three Key Traits Identified in Metahabilitated Survivors

Hope, Gratitude, and Purpose

After listening to numerous survivor stories, it is clear to me that when I hear these personal insights and ideas in their narrative—hope, gratitude, and life purpose—I have noted that, over time, they do well. I never suggest or talk about it in advance of hearing their story. I simply listen, and when I hear these traits or themes, I point out their importance, and it provides support and confidence as survivors continue their work in moving forward.

Why the Change in the Rehabilitation System?

The simple answer to that question is because survivors and their families wanted and demanded change. Over the last fifteen years, I have addressed individual survivors, their families, as well as therapists and other healthcare professionals, noting that the same despair and frustration I experienced echoed with their experiences. I am a generalist in trauma and have used the metahabilitation program to assist with multiple recovery and support groups made up of veterans, athletes, coaches, oncology patients, and their families; individuals with spinal cord and traumatic brain injuries and their families; foster youth; individuals suffering with addiction and dependency; incarcerated individuals and those on probation, as well as the clinicians helping them; family therapists, first responders, physicians, nurses, and physical, speech, and recreational therapists, to name a few. My research is the foundation for a popular college course focused on trauma and posttraumatic growth. Prior to giving lectures and speaking to groups, I begin by asking, "How many of you are aware of PTG? Or posttraumatic growth?" I would get a few raised hands, more now than a couple of years ago, but those who raise their hands are still in the minority. Time after time, individuals, families, even therapists would come to me after my presentation and ask, "How come this is the first time someone spoke to us like this?" So many survivors want to move forward, but all too often the focus is more about what is wrong than what is right, what they can't do instead of what they can and want to do, and failing to utilize a clear strategy and system that identifies and emphasizes the strengths they possess. Once described and encouraged, survivors and families actually recognize this occurrence; however, for many reasons, accentuating strengths, resilience, capacity, and a simple system they can follow to achieve these outcomes is not always prioritized when planning their care and therapy.

The system needs tweaking and a fresher attitude. Survivors and their families want and need to know *what to do* from the start. How do we/they even begin to move forward? The innovation of this system is its simplicity and core message: using pre-existing natural and personal assets and abilities, encouraging survivor hope, control and choice, and completely incorporating them in all aspects of decision and planning of their care. Metahabilitation is rooted in exposing and identifying personal control, capability, and choice (see Chapters 7 and 8). It is unique, resulting from a personal experience—my experience and my intense desire to reduce the burden and suffering of others in the aftermath of adversities and trauma and, importantly, to hold open hope for their future. I understood the basics, years of research added to and supported the knowledge, and the life experiences—the stories of very brave, hardworking survivors—filled in the rest, bringing forth a distinctive, clear strengths-based recovery pathway that guides survivors toward healing and posttraumatic growth. It starts and finishes with the survivors themselves. It is their journey, their hero's journey beginning when they take control, identify their abilities and make productive choices regarding goals, working diligently with capable and trusted support systems to get there. Again, the main impact of metahab is its distinct and intentional focus on abilities and possibilities, allowing survivors to be in control of their recovery process. This system raises expectations of how survivors can live and move forward as they work toward a positive, growth outcome. It works by using *their* dreams and aspirations, pushing them—sometimes gently, sometimes more forcefully—to *move forward*. I readily admit I don't always have the answer, but I have developed, over time, really good questions that prompt survivors to recognize and, at times, ultimately discover their resilience, power, and potential as they progress and move forward. *You got this.*

Conclusion

> *When I look back at those days I have no doubt that*
> *Providence guided us, not only across those snowfields,*
> *but across the storm—white sea that separated Elephant*
> *Island from our landing—place on South Georgia.*
> —Ernest Shackleton

As with explorer Ernest Shackleton, I feel Providence guiding and energizing my adventure and this work. Friends, family, and colleagues have provided important insights and ideas to help organize my thinking regarding direct application of the concept and process. Again, this work is not done alone; nothing worthwhile is. So many people were and still are a part of my work and the metahabilitation movement. As I look back over the last several years, I clearly see how my work, discernment, research, and life experience provided necessary parts to my message and creation of a recovery system specifically supporting resilience and growth in the aftermath of trauma and troubling events. All the coincidental meetings and conversations, films, and documentaries I watched again and again, times when I turned right instead of left, and saw a book, a sign, or went down an unplanned path—all to find unexpected messages that brought new ideas or supported existing ones. Years of these experiences, along with a fierce determination and passion to bring these ideas and behaviors forward, helped me at a very deep level to process, understand, and share this concept with other survivors and their families. This work is fundamental to my being. In Chapter 2, I shared about my opportune meeting in the hospital hallway with the cardiologist who told me I couldn't run or swim again. As if it was yesterday, I vividly remember standing in front of him and defiantly insisting, "You need to stop telling me what I can't do. I am living what I can't do. You need to tell me what I *can* do and ask me what I want to do, then your job is to help get me there." Little did he or I know, that defining moment revealed my purpose and my life's work.

I hope my efforts and that of others presented in this book impacts not only survivors, families, and friends but also influences messages given by clinicians to move away from focusing on limitations and negativity and stop minimizing survivors' potentials in the aftermath of trauma. I understand clinicians may fear providing false promises or subjecting survivors to false hopes. They may be worried the survivor may not reach certain results or have a desired outcome, but you still have to give them some type of *hope*. Who knows exactly what can and will happen? That is why medicine and nursing is referred to as art. Even the most advanced science and technology can't account for or measure the human component. You need to leave that aspect of choice open for survivors. Dr. Richard Tedeschi reminded me that we have all been taken aback or had surprises regarding how people have turned things around, and it is best that physicians, nurses, therapists, and clinicians be humble in these settings. I include myself in this group. We don't—I don't—have all the answers, but it is essential to show we care and hold open possibilities for all potentials. *You got this.*

PART FOUR

CHAPTER 10

WELLNESS AND MINDFULNESS: KEYS TO RELAXATION AND MENTAL FITNESS

*One day, in retrospect, the years of strug-
gle will strike you as the most beautiful.*
—Sigmund Freud

This book would not be complete without this chapter. This information is essential. Thus far, the many aspects of the survival experience focused on choices, control, and bringing forth growth. As I dissect the mental and emotional health of survivors, each part, each structure, needs to be supported, concentrating on what can and should be put into a daily practice to build resilience and encourage wellness and mental fitness. These practices and behaviors are not only helpful—they are vital. Utilizing even a few of these suggestions, beginning with ones you like and have used in the past, will help maintain and improve your capacity to take on everyday life challenges, reduce toxic stress, and prepare you to deal with major traumas. The following provides ideas, practices, and evidence supporting your engagement in these constructive activities.

Mindfulness

Mindfulness is commonly translated from the Pali word *sati*, meaning "to be alert"—a moment-to-moment awareness of one's surroundings and mental states. Rather than doing things mindlessly or simply out of habit, it infers actions are done consciously, *mindfully*. This state of consciousness uses specific techniques to process information, bringing forth more receptiveness and attention to life experiences. Specific and direct benefits of mindfulness are substantial. They include emotional regulation and balance, self-control, objectivity, tolerance for yourself and others, regulation of fear, improved concentration and mental clarity, stress reduction, compassionate behaviors toward oneself and others, enhanced feelings of gratitude, connecting with others, and improving internal, natural systems that support immunity and coping with stress and anxiety.[71]

It is important to remember there is no cookie-cutter approach. There are behaviors survivors share, but there are also unique aspects that must be taken into consideration when suggesting care and interventions. Working with survivors and their families over the past two decades, it is clear to me: there are similarities as well as differences in each situation, and I don't have all the answers—and that is okay. Actually, it is a good thing because I recognize how much survivors contribute to the answers. I have sound ideas based on my own experience and up-to-date clinical and behavioral scientific research, but each person is unique, each survivor's situation and how they incorporate traumatic events into their life is slightly different. I have identified

---

[71]   Davis, Daphne M., and Jeffrey A. Hayes. "What Are the Benefits of Mindfulness? A Practice Review of Psychotherapy-Related Research." *Psychotherapy*, 48, 2011.

my role as being supportive, directing my attention to formulating and asking really good questions while providing sound, well-researched evidence to help survivors and their families take control and make choices that fit and work for them. It became clear—first in my own situation and later recognizing it in others—that if you don't include them in the equation, collaborate and meet them where they are, and recognize what they identify as important, your best intentions, ideas, and interventions simply won't work. They will not be effective. Their recovery, their survival, their story is about them. Therefore, I designed and provided in this book useful and practical activities for you to consider. Choose what you like, what works, and most importantly, focus in on what you will actually do! Some of these behaviors and activities are self-evident. You might already be using them, but I want to make sure you know *why* doing them is a good idea and have clarity regarding *how* they work. Hopefully you will be inspired to improve your habits and pick up one or two new ones to try. It is up to you, but you must do something. *You got this!*

> *The art of medicine consists of amusing the*
> *patient while nature cures the disease.*
> —Voltaire

I do not want this book to be too prescriptive, ridged, or inflexible. Instead I hope you engage your internal, natural abilities brought forth by mindful and thoughtful awareness of behaviors, mental states, and developed growth mindsets. Learning from challenges, recovery itself, and growing from trauma is a journey—a lonely, solo one in many respects. As mentioned, each person brings forth unique practices and attitudes based on personal and family history, current life situations, and perceptions of desired futures. Trials and tribulations generate an awareness and understanding that most of the curative aspects of diseases and illness lie within each of us. It is built in; it is natural. Using medicine, technology, and therapies brings forth survival and healing, but capitalizing on and engaging our natural systems to support adaptation, healing, and growth through mindfulness is synergistic. Combining the strengths of both body and mind is far greater than using them separately. *You got this,* you really do. The following content provides suggestions and direction to engage and apply natural capacities to boost your physical, emotional, and mental fitness in the aftermath of trauma.

Suggestions for Mindfulness Practice

Reducing Stress and Building and Supporting Mental and Emotional Fitness

In this subtitle, I purposefully use the word "suggestions." These are offerings, recommended tools, and reminders for you to engage in healthy and productive behaviors that support your peace of mind, well-being, and help you find balance in your life. That life involves challenges, stresses, and traumas but also the potential for dealing effectively with them. Your capacity and overall success is rooted in the behaviors and perceptions you adopted regarding these events. Do you adapt and adjust, ultimately and over time accept adversities as growth opportunities and use them to your benefit? Resolve to support that mindset. Reduce chaos and stress when you can. Strengthen your response by recognizing pre-existing abilities and continue to improve your coping and adaptive skills. Finally, appreciate the utility of these life situations and commit to integrating thoughtful, mindful, and healthy techniques into your daily life (review Chapter 4: Happiness and Gratitude). These behaviors can be applied in the moment or used as strategies to guard against future threats to your safety, well-being, and mental health.

These activities contribute to your health and wellness, but again, combining them with mindfulness techniques has an additive effect, bringing forth better results. Therefore, after each suggested activity,

I provided specific examples or ways to do each mindfully. If you are already engaged in or using stress management and mindfulness practices in some form or another—great! These ideas, as well as those presented in earlier chapters (resilience, happiness, and metahabilitation), aim to support and encourage continued use of existing practices. Lastly, a gentle reminder: it is crucial to use and model these behaviors and mindsets for children. This nurturing and supportive behavior assists them during troubling times, not only revealing positive and productive coping mechanisms for them to copy, but may also positively influence gene expression and activity in the future. Use the ones you are familiar with first, then incorporate others you find interesting and potentially useful. *You got this. Now, model the way for the next generation.*

Integrating Mindfulness into All Activities

Being "consciously aware" when engaged in the following activities enhances their benefit in bringing forth wellness, relaxation, and stress reduction. For example, when engaging in physical activities, focus on how you feel internally, incorporate your surroundings, and recognize how it adds to your experience of "being." When breathing, actually think about it. Focus attention on your breathing: inhaling, exhaling, feeling the air fill your lungs and the movement of your diaphragm. Finally, as with exercise, slow down and take your time. In the forest or in any outside area that is calming (pictures can help too!), remember to breath, touch trees, see paths, and take it all in. Connect mindfully with each experience and let it feed your natural instincts and senses.

Journaling

One of the first practices suggested is journaling. Why journal? In researching this behavior, I found a few important change agents, including Albert Einstein, Leonardo da Vinci, Frederick Douglass,

Marie Curie, and Nikola Tesla all kept a journal. It allowed them to keep a record of their thoughts, feelings, and ideas by using the written word and illustrations. Concepts are laid out. Thoughts are analyzed on paper. Emotions are addressed. It is a way to keep track of your life—what has happened and how you worked through things, providing a record of your strategies and growth. You find inspiration as you think "out loud," setting goals, tracking progress, and strengthening your memory. Writing down thoughts can reduce negativity regarding events and can help you lessen stress and anxiety while you gain self-confidence. I keep mine with me. You never know when you will come upon a thought or idea that needs to be written down! Get a journal. Write down your feelings. Focus on mindfulness (words, thoughts, and emotions), mental fitness, and gratitude—all aspects that encourage self-care and personal growth.

There are some aspects of empathy and compassion
that can only be discovered through suffering.
—Lojong practice

Practicing Compassion: It Begins with You

Practicing compassion—especially self-compassion—is all too often an afterthought. However, building on the principles and practices of metahabilitation, posttraumatic growth (PTG), and mindfulness practices, self-compassion is obligatory. Recognition of others' pain, acting to help them and revealing a real, visible expression of love for those suffering is an essential life strategy. To do this effectively, it is critical that you first recognize how caring for yourself and dealing compassionately with your *own* daily challenges and suffering brings better personal health and supports your ability to love and serve others. Practicing self-compassion helps shape adversities and struggles, encourages stress resilience, supports wellness, and improves relationships, both personally and professionally.

People who struggle with self-compassion do not lack compassion, but they tend to be demanding in their personal expectations, holding themselves to very high standards. Feeling weak or inadequate if they fail to meet those standards, their frustration needs a place to rest. It is too difficult to hold onto, so it pours over onto others—affecting relationships as a presumed deficiency—and a sense of failure grows. Think about it. Do you expect too much from yourself? Do you take personal time, or have you looked at that time as a luxury that must be earned rather than as a necessity? It is critical to understand how indispensable this strategy and behavior is. When you cut yourself some slack, when you give yourself time to relax, pray, exercise, socialize, or go on vacation—something you do to take care of yourself—you can then support others and compassionately encourage them to do the same.

As I discussed earlier, exercise has become a skill and a compassionate practice for me. When I first started to build that into my life, I waited until everything else was done for the day, making sure I met all the needs of my family first. It seemed as if that time was an extravagance or a privilege. *I* came to recognize this as unhealthy. I put that on myself. When I finally stopped thinking of it in that way and instead, recognized it as a daily necessity to keep me mentally and physically healthy, I stopped judging others when they also took time for themselves. When my husband, children, colleagues, and friends took time to swim, hike, run, go to a movie, read a book, take a nap, or get a massage, *I got it.* I understood. I supported them, actually applauding the fact that they took time for themselves and reminded myself one more time that this behavior is a strength, not a weakness. Think about it as a daily medicine required to keep you from getting sick. If you have diabetes, do you consider taking your insulin as a privilege? If you have high blood pressure, is your medication a treat?

No, it is required to keep you healthy. Make these behaviors a priority, a gift for you, then give that loving gift to others.

Mindfulness in Compassion

Compassion literally means "to be one with." Whether it is for yourself or another, being present in a compassionate way recognizes that you are fully engaged in the emotion. Try this: think of a memory where you did not get a desired outcome. Now look at yourself from the outside, actually step aside in your mind and be completely present with yourself. Watch it like a movie. Notice, as you look at yourself from this perspective, how you can be more objective. You don't get swallowed up with disappointment, sadness, or anger. You can now open yourself and your heart to kindness, caring, and understanding, and move away from pain and self-criticism. Doing this allows recognition of how harshly judging yourself and beating yourself up, does not get you what you want. It becomes unproductive. Instead, use the observations and judgment to build personal resilience, grit, and growth.

The Three Indispensable Elements of Self-Compassion

Dr. Kristin Neff is an expert on self-compassion. Her work and pioneering research led to defining and applying the term and specific practice. Here are three important ideas based on her work.

Practice kindness toward yourself in difficult times.
Pay attention to your suffering in a mindful, non-obsessive way.
Common humanity: Recognize that suffer-
ing is part of the human experience.
—Kristin Neff, PhD, University of Texas, Austin

Tips for Cultivating Self-Compassion and Encouraging Wellness Practices *(Ideas from Marina Krakovsky and Dr. Joyce Mikal-Flynn)*

1. Realize "beating yourself up" and being hypercritical *does not* help you attain your goals. It is actually a deterrent and holds you back. It weakens you, making you less motivated, less emotionally stable, allowing you to fall back on excuses.

2. Resist the urge to compare. Do not put yourself in settings where judgments provoke your fear, worry you, or are obnoxious and less than helpful. This is very damaging. When I notice that I am comparing myself to other faculty members, researchers, mothers, runners, or clinicians, I can go to some very frustrating places as I sit in that dark room and continually develop negatives. I need to recognize what I am doing and get out of that ditch. If you find that you are comparing yourself to others, take time to refocus. Call a friend, meditate, or go for a walk, something to move your mind away from harsh self-judgment. There is no perfect life; no one is happy all the time. Choose instead to look at what you have, review your accomplishments, and praise others' achievements. Also, look at the commonality of life's struggles, disappointments, and traumas, then concentrate on supporting one another.

3. If the notion of self-compassion seems too frightening, it may be a result of unresolved past challenges, traumas, or abuse. Take time to take care of yourself, and consider getting counseling, preferably in compassion-focused therapy.

4. As a parent and/or teacher, realize the balance between celebrating achievements and recognizing disappointments. Bad and tough things happen in every life, including yours and your child's. Practice compassion toward your children by praising their *effort*. Outcomes are not always successes. Your

children may not always come out a winner, get a good grade, the grade they think they deserved, or make it through a particular challenging event, but recognize how they *tried*. They worked at it. Also, demonstrate behaviors that help build a growth mindset, showing children how to adapt and adjust well so they can bounce back—to *better!*

5. If you find yourself engaging in negative thoughts, behaviors, or self-criticism, stop, count to ten, then ask yourself, *what am I missing? What am I making up about the situation? Is this behavior helping me? Is this thinking productive?* Take time out and critically answer those questions. This strategy will help you "pump the brakes," slow down, and ultimately move away from self-criticism and negative thinking into a more useful, creative, purposeful mindset that brings balance, insight and control to your behaviors and life.

6. Take time for yourself. Take time for yourself. Take time for yourself. *Enough said.*

Physical Activity

We are designed to move. Whether you exercise hard or enjoy a daily walk, there is no question that physical activity allows you to feel better, live longer, and have fewer problems with intellectual, stress, and mood disorders. It provides time to process, to look inside and figure things out. Aerobic or vigorous activities in particular enhance mood and reduce the stress response for hours. Start by doing simple things, such as a daily fifteen-minute walk. Climb the stairs instead of taking the elevator. Park far from entrances to get some steps in, and try walking or riding a bike to events instead of using your car. To make these behaviors habits, you must:

1. Find something you *enjoy* doing and do it regularly. I suggest daily, but if you can't, then at least three times per week.

2. Do something that stresses you intellectually and physically, allowing you to become stronger. Your body and psyche have the capacity to respond to such exertions in a productive, growth-like manner, improving performance and future capabilities. Use it. Set goals, push yourself, but make it fun.

3. Get a "battle buddy" or friend to join you. I learned this term and practice when working with veterans. Going on hikes and camping trips, I was assigned a "battle buddy." We made each other accountable, watching over and keeping each other going. The focus is on helping one another show up, caring for each other, working together, and motivating and challenging each other. It works!

Mindfulness in Physical Activity

Exercise, or as I like to refer to it, physical activity, is fantastic but consider doing it mindfully. That will add to its positive effect. No matter what activity you choose, take time to focus and *be in the moment*, completely present in your body and spirit. *Feel* the activity. If you ride a bike, feel your feet and legs move as you cycle. If you run, feel your feet hit the pavement. Sense your breathing, your heart beating. If you row, feel the oar at the catch. Revel in the joy of your body performing the activity, how it feels to engage, be one with the motion, aware of your breathing and your heart beating. If you are outside, notice the sun, clouds, temperature, and time of day. Celebrate how you feel at the time. Be in the zone.

Spirituality

Spirituality is complex. In general, it relates to the recognition of feelings, a sense of belief that there is something greater or bigger than yourself, something more to the human experience than a sensory or physical understanding. It refers to a belief in a greater being, involving a cosmic or divine nature. It is deeply personal, focusing on internal beliefs and values and describing a private relationship with God or the divine. Religions are more extrinsic, external beliefs and practices. They are the actual demonstration, sign, or practice of a particular belief system.

When traumas occur, many times this aspect of personal identity and belief is shaken and disrupted, sometimes significantly. Attitudes regarding safety, goodness, and life's meaning in the aftermath of trauma can bring about a negative view of God, a questioning of one's spiritual identity, even losing one's fundamental spiritual values. I experienced this. When returning to a life that was significantly changed and severely challenged, I became very indignant, turning away from God and a spiritual life due to my anger and fear. Initially unable to understand *why* it happened, I shut down. It took some time, but with guidance and counseling, I came to terms with the trauma. I recognized I might never get a good answer as to *why* and realized I needed spiritual and religious support in my life if I would ever fully get through the event. I turned back, finding a positive change and a deeper spiritual connection that helped in my recovery and healing process.

Spirituality and religion can be questioned in the aftermath of trauma, but research does reveal that it can also serve as an important resource, allowing survivors to process and ultimately assimilate the event in a beneficial manner. Over time, one's faith can be strengthened, bringing forth resilience and the ability to face future life challenges. An increase in spiritual consciousness—the meaning of life and purpose, trusting and relying on a personal deity—is brought about by regular spiritual practices. These actions help allow for meaning-making, instilling a sense of hope and belonging. I leave the exact activities and practices to your discretion. It may include a collaboration of sorts that embrace more formalized religious practices, prayer, meditation, or group prayer. Whatever works for you, whatever you like, use it to your advantage.

Mindfulness in Spirituality

There can be misunderstanding with spirituality and mindfulness or meditation. There are forms of meditation that utilize prayer; however, to be *mindful* in spiritual practices, one must be present with words, deeds, thoughts, and, most importantly, actions. The focus is on how it makes you feel. Do you sense joy? Bliss? Are you calmly connected with others and your surroundings? Find specific spiritual and religious practices that comfort and inspire you to be totally mindful and present in each moment.

Socialization: Isolation Is Unhealthy

We are social beings, and community is key to our humanity and well-being. During the 2020 COVID-19 crisis, this was clearly one of the biggest problems and concerns: isolation and loneliness. You don't need to over-socialize, but if you are not spending time with friends and others outside of work, if you are detaching from family, social, church, and exercise activities on a regular basis, it is not healthy. It can even be dangerous, especially among the ranks of high-intensity professions, such as soldiers, first responders, and healthcare professionals.

I want to stress this point. I work with a lot of professions and professionals that provide services and are exposed regularly to high-level traumas and challenges in their job. They usually work in teams. Special attention is needed when there is an illness, injury, or retirement from these types of service jobs, professions, sporting (recreational, elite, and professional athletes), and other activities that take a person away from the group, team, or events they enjoyed prior to their life alteration or change. By being out of the group and no longer feeling a part of it, they not only miss the activities but also the esprit de corps, the support, special understanding, and interactions that provided emotional balance, personal insights, and resilience. These life interruptions can leave one feeling very alone, unnecessary, cut off, and, experiencing a sense of rejection, or *social pain.* Drs. Naomi Eisenberger and Matthew Lieberman (2004; 2012) studied why being excluded from or losing the ability to participate in former activities is a painful human experience that triggers anxiety, depression, and grief over their once familiar social lives and relationships, now altered or completely missing. Their research found that physical *and* social pain share underlying neural circuitry, meaning they are part of the same brain pathways. Being cut off or socially excluded for various reasons brings about a similar stressful, physiological and physical response. People who have suffered trauma and are cut off from the life and activities enjoyed prior to the illness, injury, or trauma can experience that social disconnection as both emotional *and* physical pain. Ask soldiers coming home, retiring athletes or those who are injured and can longer play, or injured/retired firefighters. These are a few examples of concerning situations. Making sure these individuals, who are used to being a part of a team, do not completely detach or isolate is crucial. Therefore, if you find friends, family members, colleagues, and others who have suffered an illness, injury, trauma—even retirement—and are regularly disconnecting from social interactions and obligations, *intervene.* Your help is needed. Assist them by helping them find a way to serve, pick up a hobby they had let go of, re-enter their former group in a different manner, or find a new group or activity. There are many creative ways to re-engage. Encourage and support counseling or therapy. Find a way to help their transition so they begin to find life purposeful again.

Mindfulness in Socialization

This may be the single most unemployed use of mindfulness. It was tough, almost impossible, to socialize in 2020 due to COVID-19. Cell phones, FaceTime, and Zoom meetings made it somewhat possible, but these are no substitute for real, in-person gatherings. As much as is permitted and possible during these troubling times, and especially in the aftermath, you must recognize that getting together is necessary. We are social beings and live in communities; that is a strength. Specifically, when gathering mindfully in social communities, certain practices and behaviors are crucial. These include listening attentively to one another, looking directly at the person speaking, and resisting the urge to interrupt or formulate what you would like to say while the other person is speaking. Be in the moment. Be on time for activities; walking in late is very distracting and takes away from the quality of awareness. Finally, consider doing thoughtful things for others, like remembering and reaching out during special dates and anniversaries of loved ones, thus consciously and mindfully reinforcing those social connections.

Mindfulness Meditation: Taming the Wandering Mind

Most meditation traditions and practices resulted from religious and spiritual practices. There are many types, and they use different strategies to help reduce stress, relieve pain, enhance relaxation, and bring forth spiritual growth. Dr. Jon Kabat-Zinn, professor emeritus of medicine and creator of the Stress Reduction Clinic and Center for Mindfulness in Medicine, Health Care and Society at the University of Massachusetts Medical School, made mindful meditation accessible and user-friendly for all. His program Mindfulness Based Stress Reduction (MBSR) provides a step-by-step method to attain positive and productive outcomes for beginners and experts. The key to being mindful is rather simple; it essentially involves being with, or aware of, what is - being in the moment. It is a state of being consciously attentive, focusing your awareness on the present, and accepting your feelings, thoughts, and bodily sensations. Being in this state doesn't mean you stop thinking. You actually become more aware, keenly noticing your space, surroundings, and thoughts, and releasing the negative, troubling ones before they take hold of you or keep you captive.

It is not unusual when beginning to meditate to get distracted and lose focus. Let me offer some tips when utilizing this coping mechanism and skill. Find a quiet location because you want little to no distractions. Get yourself in a very comfortable posture (sitting, lying down, or even walking). Focus your attention by using a word, phrase, item, object, or breathing technique(s). Do not worry about distractions; let them come and go. They may be sensory—something you hear, feel, smell, see, or taste—or they can be emotional, like getting stuck with troubling feelings, thoughts, or ruminations. Recognize these disturbances for what they are: simply distractions. If you find meditation helpful, stay with it. Practice will make perfect.

Lastly, begin slowly. Start with five minutes then increase your time weekly, trying for twenty minutes each time. Again, there are several forms, so discover what type of meditation works, what fits with you, your mindset, and daily routines, and use it. Anecdotal and scientific evidence recognizes that meditation helps lower blood pressure, reduce anxiety, decrease pain, ease depressive symptoms, and improve sleep.

Types of Meditation

There are as many as fifteen or more types of meditation. Check them all out. Here are a few. If there is one that seems interesting or useful, learn more and seek assistance to further engage in these practices.

Mindfulness: A form of meditation that urges one to remain aware and present in the moment. Focusing on one's surrounding, holding no judgement, and living in the movement. This can be done anywhere—standing in line, waiting for a train, or hiking.

Breath Awareness: Encourages and uses specific mindful breathing techniques that center and focus thoughts and feelings.

Mantra: Used in many Eastern teachings, including Hindu and Buddhist, this meditation practice uses sounds (Om), a word, or a phrase, to chant, allowing you to become more in tune with your environment, sensing deeper levels of awareness.

Movement: This can involve taking a walk in the woods, gardening, and other forms of gentle motion or movement that actively guides your thoughts and movements. It helps those who find peace in action or activities, allowing their mind to wander purposefully.

Body Relaxation: This practice encourages people to assess their bodies for areas of tension, noticing then releasing it. Starting from one's head and progressing down to their feet, muscles are relaxed, encouraged by visualizing a wave moving over their body to release tension. This is calming, sometimes used to help with sleep.

Transcendence: A spiritual form of mediation with the goal of rising above, transcending one's current state of being, and focusing on a word or series of words. Using a trained guide and a more formalized setting is particularly helpful with this type of meditation.

Sleep

Once a biological mystery, sleep has been identified as essential for health and wellness, especially when healing and in disease prevention. Think about times when you were sleep-deprived, like having a newborn, going to school *and* working, working as a first responder or another service profession with long shifts due to emergencies, and other stressful, anxious times that interfered with your ability to relax and rest. How did you feel? How did you function? Could you process information efficiently and effectively? What was your temperament like?

Sleep is absolutely necessary to your health. Being rested enhances your ability to learn, memorize, and make logical decisions. Both your body and mind need to rest, especially if you are healing from an injury or trauma. A good night's sleep improves your physical and psychological health and recalibrates emotional brain circuits, allowing you to become more cool-headed and composed. Immunity is boosted, your metabolic state is more balanced, and cardiovascular health improves with the lowering of blood pressure. Some specific and helpful suggestions for sleep include:

1. Seven to nine hours of sleep a night is needed.
2. Turn off electronics at least one hour prior to sleep to make your environment restful and calm.
3. No naps after 3:00 p.m. and no caffeine late in the day. Reduce alcohol intake and avoid nicotine.
4. Try a nice cup of warm milk and use lavender aromatherapy—they work.
5. Follow a sleep routine. This is a tough one, but it really helps. If possible, try to go to bed and wake up at the same time each day.

6. I promote *daily* physical activity because it does help you sleep but not within two to three hours of bedtime.

7. Practice makes perfect. Keep trying, and over time, you will succeed.

Mindfulness in Sleep

One might think, *how can I mindfully sleep? I am asleep!* There is more to sleeping than closing your eyes, resting, and dreaming. The depth of the rest makes a difference, so intentionally make sure the room you sleep in is set up in a manner that promotes rest, including lowering the room temperature to sixty-five degrees Fahrenheit. Try to avoid sleep aids/medicine. Practice good habits that allow you to naturally rest and relax. Be consistent with your bedtime. Go to bed and wake up at about the same time each day.

Mindfulness: A Pathway to Joy - How Can Mindfulness Be Supported and Improved?

1. Mindfulness meditation: These are self-regulatory practices focused on attention and awareness. Work to bring your mental processing under voluntary control, fostering mental well-being and developing specific capacities, including calmness, clarity, and concentration.[72]

2. Practice and journal gratitude regularly.[73]

3. Develop emotional and mental immunity. Get in the habit of practicing morning intention-setting and meditating or reciting a prayer.

---

3 Specific Daily Practices to Reduce Stress and Nurture Relaxation

Walking, Breathing Techniques and Shinrin-yoku

1. *A Daily Walk: at least twenty to thirty minutes*

2. *Breathing Techniques/Breath Therapy: practice twice daily*

   a. Focus on the Breath/Basic Mindful Breathing

   Simply focus your attention on your breath as you inhale and exhale. You can do this standing, sitting, or lying in a comfortable position.

   b. Straw Breathing

   Place a drinking straw in the center of your lips, keeping it in place by using your hand. Breathe in slowly and deeply through your nose. Then, exhale through your mouth slowly and evenly, using the straw. Repeat this technique for three to five minutes, taking time with each breath.

   c. The Complete Breath

   Sit quietly in a comfortable position. Become aware of your breathing, and as you breathe, say the word, *"JUUUST."* Then, as you breathe out, say "One." Time your breathing like a mantra. Continue for several minutes, and when you finish, sit quietly and relax for a few minutes, then open your eyes and stand up slowly.

d. Diaphragmatic Breathing/Belly or Abdominal Breathing

This breathing exercise helps strengthen an important breathing muscle, your diaphragm. Start by getting in a comfortable position—sit or lie flat. Place a hand on your abdomen just below your ribs, then place the other on your chest. Next, take a deep breath in through your nose, letting your abdomen or belly push your hand out or away. When breathing out, do it with pursed lips like you are whistling. See if you can do this at least three, maybe even ten times.

e. Alternate Nostril Breathing

Close your right nostril with your thumb, inhale through the left nostril, and at the top of the inhalation, close the left nostril and open the right nostril. Next, keep your left nostril closed and inhale through your right nostril. Repeat the process up to ten full cycles. As you get better at this process and feel comfortable, you can steadily increase that number.

3. *Shinrin-yoku: Forest Bathing*
    Enhancing relaxation by using what nature gave us

    a. *Shinrin-yoku* is a term that means "forest bathing" or taking in the forest atmosphere. It was coined in 1982 by Japan's Ministry of Agriculture, Forestry, and Fisheries, and is defined as "making contact with and taking in the atmosphere of the forest."

Background: Why This Works

For most of our millions of years of existence, we lived in the natural environment. Our body and how it functions is well-matched to natural settings, which may be the reason why such environments can increase relaxation. Shinrin-yoku involves engaging in direct contact with and taking in the forest atmosphere to encourage mental and physical relaxation. Research revealed that *engaging* in forest settings stimulates relaxation by lowering sympathetic nerve activity (flight or fight), reducing cortisol levels (stress hormone), as well as blood pressure and heart rate, while enhancing overall health and wellness. Simply walking in a forest or forested area for two to four miles decreases glucose levels (blood sugar).

Can't get out of the office or out of town anytime soon? Get a picture. This practice can still help. Even *viewing* forest landscapes can reduce your stress by lowering cortisol levels, heart rate, and blood pressure. First, try to make time in your schedule for a walk, run, or hike in a forested area. But if you can't, get an image of a forest landscape that you like to look at. It helps!

Identify Purpose and Ways to Be of Service

The mystery of human existence lies not in just staying alive, but in finding something to live for.
—Fyodor Dostoevsky

I consider this a mindful activity. Being present, being aware, and focusing on the moment and how that makes you feel includes being of service. People who do well in life, especially after struggles, disappointments, and traumas, thought through situations and found purposeful activities, ways to be of service, and opportunities to give back. They are aware—profoundly aware—of what the event meant in the past and in the now. Finding meaning in one's suffering and despair can lead to an enhanced, conscientious sense of purpose. You recognize it and feel as if you have something to offer that directly resulted from your experience. You know things now—deep, significant, and useful insights found by enduring and moving forward during some of the darkest times. These perceptions brought about nonjudgmental, conscious states of awareness that led to productive behaviors and reasons for carrying on.

These suggestions and recommended behaviors are supported by science, revealing why and how they work. There is an artful innovation and imagination in each one. I hope you will use this information to support and guide you when using these practices and incorporating these behaviors into your daily life.

Conclusion

People are disturbed not by events alone,
but by the views they take of them.
—Epictetus, philosopher

There is effective help and support as you wrestle with and move forward in the aftermath of trauma. Survivors' stories helped dissect issues, providing guidance, instructions, and strategies, revealing what to do, how to move forward, and ultimately, how to grow in the aftermath of traumas and challenges. It is essential to note that these are not just good ideas. Neuroscience, biology, psychology, and genetics tells us that effectively incorporating these behaviors into our lives enhances physical, spiritual, and mental health. Decide what works for you and integrate them, building wellness behaviors into your personal and professional life. When survivors—actually, people in general—utilize the suggested behaviors, they *are* happier, more content, and healthier.

Finally, when studying for my doctorate, which focused on leadership, one of my favorite professors told the class, "When you are a leader, it is no longer optional for you to take time out, to spend time in deep contemplation. It is a requirement of your rank." As a survivor, you can and must take control—you must be the leader in your recovery and life after. Take his advice. Contemplate what surviving well looks like. Start by taking care of yourself; take time away. Go for a walk. Play. Laugh. Take deep breaths all through the day. Create battle buddies, friendships, and other informal partnerships to support you. Make a list of people in your life who can help you discern critical junctures, sharpen your thinking, help you persevere through difficulties, and assist you in reaching the next step or the next big goal. Louis Pasteur said, "Fortune favors the prepared mind," so work on yours. Practice mindfulness, compassion, and use your imagination to help you move forward. *You got this!*

If you are struggling, it may be because you are out of balance. It is sometimes helpful to go back to the *basics*. I created a pneumonic device to easily describe this practice. Think about the word *BASICS and follow the suggested practices.*

- **B**alance work and family
- **A**cts of kindness and gratitude
- **S**pirituality
- **I**nsight into your purpose; what you can offer to the community and world
- **C**ount your blessings
- **S**ocialize; engage with family and play

Content Support:

Forest Bathing

Park, Tsunetsugu, Kasetani, Kagawa, and Miyazaki. "The physiological effects of Shinrin-yoku: evidence from field experiments in 24 forests across Japan." Environmental Health and Preventative Medicine 15, 2010. 18–26.

Park, Ishii, Furuhashi, Lee, Tsunetsugu, Morikawa, et al. "Physiological effects of Shinrin-yoku using HRV as indicator." Journal of Forest Research, 2006.

Park, Tsunetsugu, Kasetani, Hirano, Kagawa, and Sato, et al. "Physiological effects of Shinrin-yoku using salivary cortisol and cerebral activity as indicators." Journal of Physiological Anthropology 26;2, 2007. 123–8.

Mindfulness and Practices

Brown, Kirk Warren, Richard M. Ryan, and J. David Creswell. "Mindfulness: Theoretical Foundations and Evidence for its Salutary Effects." *Psychological Inquiry 18(4),* 2007. 211–237.

Davis, Daphne M., and Jeffrey A. Hayes. "What Are the Benefits of Mindfulness? A Practice Review of Psychotherapy-Related Research." *Psychotherapy 48(2),* 2011. 198–208.

Lama, Dalai and Howard C. Cutler. *The Art of Happiness.* Riverhead, 1998.

Lama, Dalai, Desmond Tutu, and Douglas Carlton Abrams. *The Book of Joy: Lasting Happiness in a Changing World.* Penguin Random House, 2016.

Schweikert, Catherine W., PA-c, MPH, Doctoral Candidate in Applied Psychophysiology.

Breathing Techniques and Practices

Howard, Dr. Kent. Mindfulness and Stress Reduction (program paper), *Institute for National Resources (INR)*. 2018.

Social Isolation

Eisenberger, Naomi I., and Matthew D. Lieberman. "Why rejection hurts: A common neural alarm system for physical and social pain." *Trends in Cognitive Sciences, 8(7),* 2004. 294–300.
Eisenberger, Naomi I. "The pain of social disconnection: Examining the shared neural underpinnings of physical and social pain." *Nature Reviews. Neuroscience, 13(6),* 2012. 421–434.

Sleep Practices

Walker, Matthew. Why we sleep: Unlocking the power of sleep and dreams, first edition. Scribner, 2017.

Spirituality

Bryant-Davis, T., Monica U. Ellis, E. Burke-Maynard, N. Moon, Pamela A. Counts, and G. Anderson. "Religiosity, Spirituality, and Trauma Recovery in the Lives of Children and Adolescents." *Professional Psychology: Research and Practice, 43(4),* 2012. 306–314.
Drescher, Kent D., Gilbert Ramirez, Jeffrey J. Leoni, Jennifer M. Romesser, Jo Sornborger, and David W. Foy. "Spirituality and Trauma: Development of a Group Therapy Module." *Group, 28(4),* 2004. 71–87.

CHAPTER 11

CONCLUSION: HOW SURVIVORS ARE BUILT; *YOU GOT THIS*

Nothing else in the world...not all the armies...
is so powerful as an idea whose time has come.
—Victor Hugo

The idea that resilience, grit, and growth result from adversity, crises, and trauma is an idea and behavior that has been observed and documented for centuries. This is not an idea whose time has come but more of an idea whose time has come *back*. I believe this to my core and have seen it over and over again personally, professionally, and historically. Films, plays, books, poems, and documentaries have recognized and profiled this capacity of the human spirit. There may be some who differ, disagree, even criticize this ideology and philosophy, but there is no question it happens everywhere in the biophysical world. Species, including humans, are built to be strong, to withstand challenges and trauma, and—even more importantly—they are fashioned to *use* such events and situations to become more powerful and better able to resist future troubling and distressing situations. It sounds irrational and even scary, but people can do really well over time when things go very badly. We are built with this capacity in mind. We grow as a result of our problems; we get hurt, sometimes significantly, and we suffer. None of this is fun; much of the time it is very distressing—if not horrible. It is not something we asked for or sought out, but it happens and we must respond, beginning with surviving. Resilience, grit, and growth emerge. But as I have stated, it does not occur overnight, it takes time. How long depends on various factors, including choices you make, control you take, and the support you have in your healing and recovery process.

You don't always choose the event, but
you get to choose the response.
—Joyce Mikal-Flynn

Beyond opinions and good ideas, this book uses first person accounts and up-to-date science to help you recognize how strong you are, identify systems you have that support that strength—as well as your survival and growth—and steps to take using your past troubling events to make you hardier and more resistant to future problems. Revealing this capacity and illuminating the structure of a survivor is this book's focus: detailing how survivors used challenges and struggles as training and preparation to take on more significant and critical events; recognizing them as opportunities for insight and mental-fitness development; and demonstrating over time how to bounce back from adversity and *thrive*. Stories were provided to help you appreciate, through the lenses of others, how choosing your response, taking control of situations, and finding purpose, supported by a faith and a hope in yourself, is foundational and *key* to this process.

Surviving is the first step. Choosing the direction, the path you want to take is the critical next step. You must use these events and manage the outcome you want. You can bounce back. You can become *better*, not in spite of life's mishaps, struggles, and traumas but as a direct result of them. Again, it is not easy. It is rough, sometimes dangerous stuff. But over time, the frustration, pain, even the suffering you endured can and does bring forth wisdom, meaning, insight, and an inner strength that supports you, becoming the fertile field on which you will grow. As I do with my students and patients, I want you to stop and take a moment. Think about a life event, a challenge, struggle, or even a traumatic situation in which you survived and became stronger. Now, recognize how this event made you better, more confident, more compassionate, and helped you find your life purpose.

Tom Clancy, author of complicated, fascinating literary works, such as *The Hunt for Red October*, *Clear and Present Danger*, and *Patriot Games*, was quoted as saying, "I do not over-intellectualize the production process. I try to keep it simple: Tell the damned story." This book tells how survivors are built and reminds you of your capacity to grow after trauma. Give yourself credit. You are much stronger than you realize. Sometimes you have your finest hour as you deal with troubling situations, and other times, like me, you failed—you fell. Those times, as well as lesser challenges, are tests and opportunities to mentally, emotionally, and physically prepare for the big ones. You have a story. Don't forget it. *You got this*. Believe in yourself, then give that gift to others. This is the anatomy of a survivor and that's the "damned story" I wanted and needed to tell.

APPENDICES

APPENDICES

METAHAB CORE VALUES

Supporting the Principles and Practice of the Metahabilitation Recovery System

- Trauma is a universal experience.
- A survivor is a meaning-seeking, physical, and spiritual being.
- Prior to a traumatic event or crisis, one may lack self-knowledge, understanding, and self-awareness, underestimating their personal potentialities.
- Trauma and crisis allow the chance to face fears and presumed limitations.
- Trauma/crisis present profound opportunities to fully learn who we are and, more importantly, who we can be.
- Trauma, challenges, and struggles are opportunities to transform and evolve.

The above statements were first developed in 2009. Over time, using ongoing research, and works from Drs. J.F. Bugental and Tom Greening, as well as extensive experience with survivors, families, and clinicians, I refined them, providing more clarity and accuracy regarding my beliefs and the foundation of my practice.[74,75]

1. Human beings have the potential and capacity for resilience.
2. Evidence for resilience and growth in the aftermath of trauma is found extensively in the evolutionary and biophysical world.

3. Major trauma and personal life crises disrupt an individual's status quo necessitating adjustments of biological homeostasis and self-concept to effectively address the disequilibrium.

4. Human beings possess the ability to adapt and become stronger when faced with severe disruptions or risks to their homeostasis.

5. Such profound existential experiences provide human beings opportunities for significant physical, intellectual and spiritual growth.

6. Human beings innately are, or can become, goal-oriented, possessing an awareness of their power to influence events, seek life meaning and creatively reconstruct their future.

SIX STAGES OF METAHABILITATION© AND SHORT DESCRIPTIONS

Stage One: Acute Recovery

Initial treatment, focused on survival and sustaining life.

Stage Two: Turning Points—Saying Yes to Life

In the midst of struggles, survivors make a firm decision to move forward.

Stage Three: Treatments—Conventional & Complementary

Survivors and their families continue to move forward, researching, seeking out and participating in various treatments.

Stage Four: Acceptance and Adaptation—A Time to Reflect.

After a busy time, survivors adapt and adjust, taking time to think about and consider aspects of their life and the changes that have occurred.

Stage Five: Reintegration—Returning to Life.

One moves back into life—at times back to what they left, other times, they move in a completely different direction…but they move forward.

Stage Six: MetaHabilitation—Taking on the Future.

This stage is ongoing. While a problematic and significantly traumatic experience occurred, an insightful, resilient, growth mindset developed. Survivors evolved. They found purpose and ways to give back.

10 ESSENTIAL TAKEAWAYS: 10 THINGS DR. JMF WANTS YOU TO REMEMBER

I am a college professor teaching courses in neuroscience, leadership, and trauma-informed care (posttraumatic growth). Since I started teaching several years ago, I thought a lot about what students would actually take away and use in their personal and professional lives. I didn't want my classes to be a "check off the box, got that one done" course. I wanted to make them matter. I am passionate about education, and I know that it is necessary to connect formal information with real-life experiences to make it more meaningful and useful. I wanted to make those connections, using what I teach in each of these courses, so I created *a Dr. JMF Top 10 Essential List of Ideas and Behaviors* for my students. I suggest you keep these in mind and take them forward, allowing you to be a thoughtful and productive person and citizen.

Beginning this lecture on the final day of class, I start by saying to students, "There will be some things you remember from this course and some you won't, but as a thoughtful, productive person and responsible member of society, let me share ten ideas and essential behaviors you can take forward to make *your* life better, as well as those you serve and live with." I want to share them with you as well so I expanded on them for this book. Some of these I learned from my parents and grandparents, some from my formal education and life experience, and some from the many courageous trauma survivors who shared their experiences and stories with me.

1. **Practice Good Manners.** This is not simply knowing what fork to use or when to open a door for someone. Practicing good manners tells others "you are important, you matter, and this event means something". It shows and communicates respect.

2. **Read, especially the classics.** I understand there is not much leisurely reading during school, but when you can, take time to *read*, especially the classics. Pick some favorites and enjoy. They will make you smarter and help you build a better vocabulary.

3. **Life is *not* about you.** This doesn't mean you are not important or that you don't matter. It simply recognizes that as we mature, we learn that the world doesn't revolve around us and our needs. We are actually happier when we understand this concept and idea. We are here to be of service to one another. Learning things and acquiring skills and abilities allows you to help others, and that is what makes you joyful. Take time to intentionally do acts of kindness. Come out of yourself; laugh at yourself. Focus less on what you want and more on the needs of others.

4. **Honor your responsibilities.** This is so important. *Show up prepared.* Be present for class, family functions, and events, and be on time. It means so much to others, and it is a sign, a gesture, that shows you care.

5. **Think first, then act. Remember your frontal lobe.** "Count to ten" is not just a fun saying. It works. You have an emotional *fight and flight* part of your brain, which is a good thing, but it needs to be ruled by your frontal lobe, your executive brain. So, when you are getting ready to deliver the best speech you wish you never made or send that nasty email, count to

ten. Let your emotions settle, then act intelligently, wisely, and with compassion.

6. **Successes are fun and should be celebrated. Failures and mistakes are valuable.** They are life's fertile soil in which to grow and become better, to get it right next time. I tell my students, "Don't tell me you made a mistake, take responsibility and tell me instead, 'I created an opportunity to improve, and I will fix it.' Then tell me your plans." The entire tone of the situation changes and opens up the growth mindset, an opportunity to get better. I also remind students that if they have not fallen flat or run up against significant obstacles in their life, they aren't trying very hard. You will never recognize your full potential unless you push yourself. If you have a hard time doing it for yourself, find someone to help push you. A coach of Wayne Gretzky, frustrated that he didn't score in an important game, told him, "You miss one hundred percent of the shots you never take." Be brave, take *good* risks, and be willing to fail. It will make you so much stronger.

7. **Exercise your mind, body, and soul daily.** Our mind and body connect; we have control of our thoughts and behaviors. Each of these three aspects of our being needs to be attended to and fostered to get the best out of them. Take time and attend to each of these areas and support all areas of growth and development.

8. **Money can make you happy.** Are you surprised to read that? Let me clarify what this means. Research reveals money can make you happy *but only if* you don't make it a priority, you use it on life experiences like education and travel, and you spend time giving it away.

9. **Be grateful.** Spend time focusing on what you have, not what you don't. Brain research tells us that thinking of three things to be grateful for prior to bedtime will help you sleep better. So, try it. There is really no downside to practicing gratitude.

10. **Find purpose and a way to serve.** Albert Schweitzer (1875–1965), a theologian, writer, humanitarian, philosopher, and physician, especially known for his missionary and healthcare work in Africa, said, "The only ones among you who will be really happy are those who will have sought and found how to serve."This is an absolute; it is a must. Especially with trauma survivors - it is a game changer. Even after going through some of the most horrific life situations, without question, *every* survivor I have interviewed who experienced growth after trauma eventually identified a purpose and found a way to *give back*. Don't make it complicated, just find things in your day-to-day life that are helpful to others. Make it a practice to be of service.

These ten ideas are basically common-sense behaviors. More than likely, you have received this advice in the past. They revolve about three basic life principles and practices that I emphasize in this book. First, develop positive coping skills and a strong, positive attitude toward life and yourself; next, take *calculated* risks; and finally, learn how to love—first yourself then others.

With Appreciation,
Dr. JMF

JOURNAL: BEGIN WITH THESE QUESTIONS

I mentioned in this book how important and useful journaling can be. I highly recommend you to take time to journal and think about these questions first, then just write. Answer them openly and honestly. Use your journal as a tool for self-knowledge, understanding, and personal growth. Answer questions, write down thoughts and ideas that come to you, as well as your successes, failures, and struggles. Reread from time to time. Recognize your growth and progress.

1. *When did you experience and overcome an adversity, disappointment, or trauma?*
2. *What did you learn about yourself? What meaning did it bring to your life?*
3. *Describe exactly how you got through it? What helped? What were the obstacles?*
4. *What did you learn about life? What about your life?*
5. *How could this, or how did this, event become useful or strengthen you?*
6. *Did the event reveal purpose? Open a new door?*
7. *Did you experience gratitude? Describe it.*
8. *Can you recognize a specific opportunity that this suffering, trauma, or adversity has given you?*

9. *Take time and identify your perceived personal strengths and support systems. What do you have? List them now and make plans to expand on them.*

10. *Finally, focus on those perceived personal strengths and support systems, continue working on expanding and improving them, and consider adding new ones to your prior list or repertoire.*

ABOUT THE AUTHOR

Author Photo: Rudy Meyers

Dr. Mikal-Flynn received her Bachelor of Science in Nursing from the University of San Francisco, a Nurse Practitioner Certificate from the University of California, Davis, and her Master's of Science in Nursing at Sacramento State University, publishing the thesis: "A Phenomenological Investigation of Near-Death Event Survivors." She completed her Doctor of Education with a dissertation entitled: "Transforming Life Crisis: Stories of Metahabilitation After Catastrophic Life Events."

A marathoner and triathlete, in 1990 she survived a sudden-death event requiring twenty-two minutes of CPR to return to life. Already a nurse practitioner and dismayed at the focus of her recovery and what was presented in the aftermath of her trauma, her mind emphasized the negative, painting a bleak future. However, her master's and doctoral research focused on posttraumatic growth (PTG) and she created a strengths-based clinical pathway guiding survivors toward a productive recovery and PTG. Her first book was *Turning Tragedy Into Triumph: Metahabilitation: A Contemporary Model of Rehabilitation*, which profiled survivors and detailed a pathway toward PTG. Her work and research continue involving how trauma affects families and communities and recognizing how they experience PTG. A Professor at CSUS, she speaks nationally and internationally on trauma, focusing on resilience and PTG. With multiple publications, her work and research continue to provide strength and hope for those who suffer in the aftermath of trauma.